This Mortal Puts On Immortality

A new unraveling of
*the mysteries of
Revelation 4, 5 & 6*

Patricia Baird Clark

Dedicated to all those who long for a deeper walk with God and are willing to forsake all worldly things in order to fulfill God's divine purpose for their life—to come into the fullness of Christ.

This Mortal Puts On Immortality
Copyright © 2016 by Patricia Baird Clark

ISBN 978-0-9818814-4-7

Other titles by the author:

Restoring Survivors of Satanic Ritual Abuse
Sanctification in Reverse
The Four Living Creatures
The Two Witnesses Prepare the Bride
Discerning of Spirits in Revelation 9
Dissociation Revealed and Healed in Scripture

All rights reserved. No part of this book may be reproduced or transmitted in any form or by any means without written permission of the author except as provided by USA copyright law.

Cover Design by Johnny Eckerman

His Presence Publishers
P.O. Box 2
Atlanta, NY 14808

www.HisPresenceOnline.org

Table of Contents

Introduction 1

Chapter One 1
    The Door Opens

Chapter Two 15
    A Different Way of Seeing

Chapter Three 31
    Our Natural and Spiritual Bodies

Chapter Four 53
    Who Is on the Throne?

Chapter Five 63
    Who Can Know My Heart?

Chapter six 77
    Removing the Sin Nature

Chapter Seven 93
    Heaven Is with Us

Chapter Eight 115
    The White Horse and His Rider

Chapter Nine 127
    The Red and Black Horses

Chapter Ten 145

Death Comes to Death

Chapter Eleven 163
    Waiting

Chapter Twelve 175
    The Transformation of Our DNA

Chapter Thirteen 199
    The Great Army in Joel

Chapter Fourteen 215
    An Army Unlimited

Appendix 229
    Verses and Interpretations

Works Cited 247

About the Author 249

Introduction

As a Christian living in the end times you have an opportunity to enter into the glories of God's kingdom even while on earth—an opportunity that was not available to even the greatest saints of past ages. The Book of Revelation that begins with John on the Isle of Patmos (with Patmos meaning "mortal") ends with him seeing the New Jerusalem, a place of immortality, which has come down out of heaven. The process of going from mortality to immortality is revealed through an inward interpretation of the Book of Revelation. Revelation when outwardly interpreted shows great destruction on the earth, but when interpreted inwardly it reveals how God will bring his people into absolute perfection. These two things will be happening at the same time as we progress deeper into the events of the end times.

This New Jerusalem is even now descending from heaven onto the earth but spiritual eyes are required to see it. I have seen it and am entering into it more and more each day. This has only been possible because the tangible presence of Jesus came to me in February of 1997 and has never left. "Tangible" is from the Latin *tangere* which simply means something that can be touched or felt. I feel his presence constantly and his touch many times a day. Jesus wants to come to all his people in this way. He allowed me to experience this initially so I could discover it in the Scriptures and write about it. In this way, others will understand what is happening when they have this experience.

When the presence of Jesus comes to you in this way, he will communicate with you many times a day. Through this communication you will have a constant awareness of his great love for you and also his loving judgment of all that you think and do. This will bring you to a depth of perfection that has never before been possible. All you need to do is hear and obey. God will do the work in you that will ultimately bring you to perfection and full redemption of spirit, soul, and body.

In this book you will see every verse in Revelation 4, 5 and 6 interpreted inwardly and allegorically consistent with the entirety of Scripture. The truths for the end times are thus revealed in context as each verse ties in with the next such that the entire revelation is gradually unfolded as only the Holy Spirit could orchestrate. Along with this I give my own experience as related to each new truth revealed in the Scripture.

We, as the people of God, must enter into this high place he has made for us to dwell in as the catastrophic events of the end times unfold because this will be the only place of safety. This high place does exist and it has been lovingly prepared for us, but it is up to us to enter. This will require letting go of our preoccupation with worldly pleasures and interests to pursue the pleasure of God's presence and the interesting things he has to reveal to us in his Word. In this way we can be in the world but not of the world. We can walk above the disasters of life on this earth even though we are physically still here. This is what it means to be seated in heavenly places with Christ Jesus. Here is what Art Katz had to say about this in his wonderful work entitled *Apostolic Foundations*:

> God intended that those made in His image would live in the reality of heaven, even while on the earth. They are on it but they do not dwell in it. When the smoke clears at the very end of the age, in the eschatological climax, there will only be two species of mankind to be found on earth, and it has nothing to do with race, but with earth or heaven. Those who dwell in the earth, whose hearts fail them for fear of the things that shall be coming upon the earth—for that is all they know and all they look for and expect. All of their values are established in it. They are earthlings—and the other group are those who dwell in heaven. They may be on the earth, but it is not their place of habitation. Earth is not where they reside, but the place where they serve. Most of us as Christians are earthlings, moored in the earth, so bound by its gravitational tug, so connected by soulish ties of affection and investment in the earth. It will take a wrench of soul to ascend up into the heavenly place. (Katz)

Encourage yourself with the truths revealed in the following pages to enter into this high place in God such that when "the smoke clears" you will not be one whose heart fails you for fear.

Chapter One

The Door Opens

In February of 1997 I had an experience with God that opened the Book of Revelation to me and forever changed my life. It happened late at night just after I had gone to bed. I was still fully awake but relaxed and waiting for sleep to come. Suddenly the presence of God came to me in a powerful way that was incredibly gentle and sweet. This presence has never left. I will describe what happened and has continued happening since in the context of Revelation 4, 5 and 6. It is important for others to know about this because I believe his presence will be coming soon in this way to every true believer. It is my intent that this book will inspire you, give you hope and prepare you to more fully understand what is happening when the Lord reveals himself to you in this way.

The Book of Revelation is about our taking off mortality and putting on immortality (1 Cor 15). It begins with John on the Isle of Patmos, with Patmos meaning "mortal," and ends with the New Jerusalem, a place of immortality, coming down out of heaven to earth. Putting off mortality and putting on immortality begins with a change experience that happens in the twinkling of an eye—in a moment—but is followed by a process wherein we put off mortality and put on immortality. Each chapter of Revelation reveals a different aspect of how this will transpire.

The Book of Revelation was written in such a way that no one could understand it unless God gave them the keys and led them through the open door. God has given me keys and taken me through the door. He has now released me to write a book about this experience and the revelations he has shown me.

I am certain it will surprise you. It isn't anything at all that any human mind could possibly have deduced no matter how diligently they studied, how thoroughly they understood Greek or how high their intelligence quotient was. It could only be understood after one has gone through the door, and one must be led through the door by Jesus when he deems it is time. This is part of the second coming.

It is my prayer that what you read on the pages of this book will utterly thrill you and give you hope and encouragement to know that our precious Lord will also take you through this door and prepare you to face the total disintegration of life as we have known it on earth if you are willing to lay down your self-life in order to seek God and allow him to dwell in you in his fullness.

Before we delve into Revelation Four, we need to understand that there are certain keys we must use to uncover this revelation. They are as follows:

Key #1 – Inward not outward: Rather than only reading the Bible as an historical account of what happened outwardly in the world, begin to read it as revealing the inward workings of the human soul and spirit. (The kingdom of God is within you, [Luke 17:21].) This leads us to…

Key #2 – Allegory. Studying the Bible allegorically was first taught by the early Church Fathers…men like Augustine, Ambrose, Jerome and Gregory the Great to name

The Door Opens

a few. Principles for allegorical study are revealed in their writings. However, it is much easier to read these principles in *Types in Genesis* by Andrew Jukes where many of these principles are explained and illustrated.

Key #3 – Numbers. We will not understand the deeper message in Scripture if we interpret numbers literally (numerically). All numbers have a spiritual meaning based on their usage throughout the entire Bible. The spiritual interpretation of numbers found in this book are from *Number in Scripture* by E. W. Bullinger.

Key #4 – Word definitions. We need to use a good exhaustive concordance to learn the original Greek or Hebrew word that lies behind the English word the translators chose.

* * * * * * * * * * * * * * * * * * * *

Chapter Four begins with the words, "After this," which refer to what has transpired in the previous chapters. For my inward view, the activity of chapters two and three, rather than being viewed as an historical account, has been the dealing of the Lord with the soul of an individual over many years of a believer's walk with God. Actually I view it as showing the process of sanctification. When we pray, read and study the Word, the Holy Spirit speaks to us convicting us of sin (" I have this against you") or confirming us of righteousness ("I know your works"), until we come to a level of maturity determined by the Lord where we are ready for the opening of the door.

Rev 4:1 After this I looked, and, behold, a door was opened in heaven: and the first voice which I heard was as it were of a trumpet talking with me; which said, Come up hither, and I will show thee things which must be hereafter.

We cannot help but read this verse and imagine it according to our own earthly understanding. I know what a trumpet sounds like. I can imagine words spoken with a voice that sounds like a trumpet. Trumpets are usually loud and can be piercingly high. It almost seems a little scary that one could hear something like that speaking out of another realm. I would imagine heaven having harps and soft flute sounds. However, the kind of hearing John is describing here has nothing to do with our natural ears. This is entirely new. This is spiritual hearing that doesn't require a certain language, e.g. English, French, German, etc. be spoken. This language is perceived in an entirely different way because it is "like a trumpet."

When we look at the Greek word for "trumpet," *sal'-pinx*, we find it is defined as "through the idea of quavering or reverberation; a trumpet." The key here is found in the similar words of "quavering" and "reverberation." Webster's Dictionary defines "quaver" as "tremble." Tremble denotes movement back and forth. Reverberation also has to do with back and forth movement made by sound waves in the air. When I describe my experience of going through the open door, you will see that it involves repeated, undulating movement although the movement is not fast as one would expect in the words "tremble" or "reverberation."

When I went through this door on February 11, 1997, and experienced this feeling of movement, I received a message that was as loud and piercingly clear as a trumpet blast and yet absolutely silent at the same time. I knew that Jesus had come to me in a special way and I knew I was deeply loved. No specific words reached the tympanic membrane of my ears, and yet I had never understood anything more clearly in all my life. And this voice of a trumpet has never stopped talking to me in this silent language since the beginning of this experience in 1997.

My Experience

On February 11, 1997 a close and very prophetic friend of mine had, in my presence, a vision of Jesus and me together in a lovely meadow. We were sitting on a large rock talking. Jesus reached down and touched my feet and said, "These feet will never touch the earth again." I had no idea what that meant.

That night as I was lying in bed all relaxed and waiting for sleep to come, I began to feel a very pleasant, rhythmic, tingling sensation in my feet that worked its way up my legs and spread out over my entire body including my arms, hands and fingers in just a few seconds. I immediately related it to the vision earlier that day where Jesus touched my feet and said they would never touch the earth again.

Due to the things the Holy Spirit was showing me in his Word, I was aware that I had not only a physical body but also a spiritual body that I would live in when I no longer needed my earthly body. I knew this spiritual body was with me but was in a dormant state as though asleep. As I felt this gentle, wave-like movement deep inside, I knew I was feeling my spiritual body being awakened. Because it started in my feet, I immediately identified it with my friend's vision. I knew Jesus had touched me in a distinct and heretofore unknown way. It was a personal and most wonderful experience which is difficult to describe. The feeling has never left but has only intensified. Because this is a spiritual experience, it is hard to describe in words. Now I understand why so much of the Bible is written as allegory. There would be no other way to explain spiritual things except by relating them to natural things we understand.

I will attempt to describe the feeling of the spiritual body being awakened by Jesus. It is a very gentle, slow rhythmic feeling almost like a deep massage but it doesn't touch the skin. It is deep inside and it gives the feeling of being deeply loved. Every fiber of my being feels loved. It is like bobbing up and down on a raft resting upon gentle waves like one would experience in a bay perhaps or one of the Great Lakes. Ocean waves would be too strong. These are gentle waves. They never, ever stop…not for one second. I cannot tell my physical body from my spiritual body because my whole being feels this wonderful sense of God's love and quickening. It is deeply relaxing and comforting.

I know I am never alone because I am able to feel God's love at all times. It is a most wonderful and amazing experience and a necessary one for what we are about to experience as the Antichrist spirit begins his overt attempt to take over the world. No matter what is going on around us, this knowledge that we are loved and we are not alone never leaves.

It also brings an understanding that we have entered into the supernatural realm. Things will never be the same. Part of us has risen above the earthly realm and heaven is very near. This is the realm we will need to live in as our world crumbles around us.

We know by this event that we are in the end times. This is not something experienced by the saints of bygone years. This is a new experience and one reserved for this particular time in history. It is part of the events of the return of Jesus for his bride. God never does things the way we think he will. This experience came as a total surprise to me.

As I was writing this I received a phone call from my daughter who lives in another state. She wanted to tell me the dream she had had early that morning. I was amazed to see that her dream was an illustration of what I had just been writing about our spiritual body.

The Dream

She and her husband and their pastor were sitting in straight-backed chairs in an empty room. She looked around the room and noticed a door. Beside the door there were some black marks that she knew should not be there. They got up, opened the door and walked through. On the other side was a secret room. It was very, very large and had openings on either side of one wall that indicated there was more room even than she was seeing. Off to one side was a master bedroom. It was large and exquisitely furnished and decorated.

Interpretation

The room they are sitting in represents the house they live in now…their natural body. It is empty except for the simple chairs they are sitting on. This means it has been cleaned out and there are no idols or any excess baggage that would hinder them as they move forth spiritually. They have been willing to forsake everything. They are sitting, symbolizing that some measure of spiritual rest has come into their lives. The pastor's presence there means that this dream has to do with their spiritual life of which the church is the focal point. (The family is growing rapidly in their new church and have availed themselves of every opportunity for growth offered there. The growth I have observed in them is phenomenal.)

The door represents the door I have been writing about in this book on Revelation 4. The black marks seen around the door represent some small sins in their lives that still need to be dealt with, but they don't have to be perfect to go through this door. They get up and walk through the door. The secret room is their spiritual body that they don't know about. It is very vast because it is in the spirit realm. The master bedroom is the bridal chamber. This confirms to me what I have thought for a long time and that is, that soon the bridegroom will come, not to be seen in the clouds in the sky, but a personal coming that is secret and silent to the faithful ones. Those who are truly seeking a relationship with Jesus and are casting aside their idols will have a "through the door" experience such as I am describing here in this book.

A New Language of Heaven

This scripture states this was "the first" voice he heard speaking. The word "first" in Greek also means "beginning." This was just the beginning of the new way of communication, a new language of heaven that I was beginning to "hear" when my spiritual body was awakened.

Come up hither, and I will show thee things which must be hereafter. This experience of the spiritual body being awakened was indeed an open door as it was just the beginning of many things Jesus would be disclosing to me through this new language. I began to hear him "speak" to me through my awakened body in a way that enabled me to hear him distinctly and clearly. When God speaks in the way I will be describing throughout this book, we will no longer have to wonder whether what we are thinking is from God or just our own thoughts. We will know beyond any doubt that God has spoken to us and we can count 100 percent on what he has said.

An important part of this new communication will be to refine our walk of holiness. There will be a continuation of what was transpiring in the previous chapters where Jesus spoke saying "I have this against you," or "I know your works." This will come to us in a way that is unmistakable. There will be more about this in later verses.

Verse and Interpretation

Rev 4:1 *After this I looked, and, behold, a door was opened in heaven: and the first voice which I heard was as it were of a trumpet talking with me; which said, Come up hither, and I will show thee things which must be hereafter.*

After having had many experiences in the church that had developed maturity in my life (after this), I had a totally new experience opened to me that was not of this earth (door opened in heaven). All over my body I began to feel a gentle, slow vibration that was so deep within I knew it was the awakening of my spiritual body (voice of a trumpet). I knew of a certainty that I had received a direct communication from God (voice of a trumpet) in that Jesus had come to me and opened to me a realm in God that had been reserved for his church of the end times (come up hither and I will show thee things which must be hereafter).

* *

Rev 4:2 *And immediately I was in the spirit; and, behold, a throne was set in heaven, and one sat on the throne.*

And immediately I was in the spirit... This experience I have just related happened suddenly and quickly. One moment I was just lying relaxed in my bed and the next this tingly, deep, rhythmic movement began in my feet and quickly spread up my legs and all over my body.

And behold, a throne was set in heaven, and one sat on the throne. The first thing I became aware of was the understanding that my spiritual body had been awakened. This is where the throne comes in. The first thing he became aware of in this verse was a throne. My experience parallels this verse because, as I will show very clearly from the scriptures, our spiritual body is God's throne. The Spirit of God had come to rest on me in a way that I was able to perceive. God had come to sit on his throne.

By now you have learned that this experience of knowing is quite different from our natural, earthly way of knowing. Yes, we do know some things on earth by feeling, but mostly we gain knowledge about something by seeing it with our natural eyes or hearing it with our natural ears. Remember the story of Helen Keller who was blind and deaf from infancy? I'll never forget the scene in the movie, *The Miracle Worker*, where her teacher, Annie Sullivan, finally succeeded in communicating with her for the first time when Helen understood the word "water" through touch. I can't see God with my natural eyes. I can't hear him with my natural ears, but he communicates directly to me through touch.

Some of the words in Revelation 4 associated with using our eyes, words such as "behold" *idou,* and "looked" *eido* also mean in Greek "to understand, to know." Another word for "look" means "to gaze, sight." As we come to understand God's communication via touch, we are to gaze at him with our imagination. This is more fully developed in my book, *The Four Living Creatures*. Now let's look at a few scriptures about God's throne:

> But the Lord shall endure for ever: he hath prepared his throne for judgment. And he shall judge the world in righteousness (Psa 9:7,8a).

How would God prepare his throne? Would he gather gold, platinum, silver, and precious stones? Would he have someone, perhaps a few angels, do some elaborate engraving on it? Maybe he would like a big, soft cushion covered in red velvet, or perhaps purple as a symbol of his majesty. No, I think not. God is preparing people. He is preparing us because as 1 Corinthians says:

> Do ye not know that the saints shall judge the world? and if the world shall be judged by you, are ye unworthy to judge the smallest matters? Know ye not that we shall judge angels? How much more things that pertain to this life?(1 Cor 6:2,3).

I hope we can all see that God is not preparing a piece of furniture. God is preparing people, and he will judge the world through us. This judgment will be a perfect judgment, not of man's understanding, but of God's perfect standard of righteousness because we will be with him on his throne:

> To him that overcometh will I grant to sit with me in my throne, even as I also overcame, and am set down with my Father in his throne (Rev 3:21).

I will explain more about the throne in Revelation 5. (My first inclination when writing about Revelation 4 was to make a series of small booklets based on each chapter in Revelation. However, I have since chosen to put my writings on Revelation together in books. I had a far greater revelation of the throne while writing Revelation 5, but in context I thought it best to leave them as is.) Here is another throne scripture from Psalms:

> God reigneth over the heathen: God sitteth upon the throne of his holiness (Psa 47:8).

Can a piece of furniture possess the quality of holiness? We could interpret the word "throne" here to mean "his authority," as in he is able to judge because his authority is based in his holiness, but the Hebrew word "throne" here actually means 'covered,' i.e. a throne (as canopied):-seat, stool, throne." Our spiritual body is covered by our natural body. Very soon in my interpretation of Revelation 4, we shall learn about the natural body and its relationship to the spiritual body and the Godhead.

God Sits on His Throne

Rev 4:2 states that this throne was "set" in heaven. In Greek this word for "set" *keimai* in the middle voice means "to lie outstretched." My spiritual body can lie outstretched. I was in bed in that position the first time I felt the Lord in this new way as my spiritual body was awakened. The word for "sat" means to "remain, to dwell, to reside." The feeling of his presence coming has never left since that experience over nineteen years ago as of this writing. He came to remain, to dwell and reside with me. However, something

The Door Opens

very special happens when I lie outstretched anywhere...be it in bed, on a couch, or on the floor. Whenever I am in that position, I feel his presence descending on me like the most lightweight blanket imaginable. He ever so gently just descends on me. I know he has never left, but I feel him sitting down on his throne whenever I am in that position! The next verse will show us more.

Verse and Interpretation

Rev 4:2 And immediately I was in the spirit; and, behold, a throne was set in heaven, and one sat on the throne.

Immediately I had been lifted up into a spiritual realm (I was in the spirit). My spiritual body (throne) was in a heavenly dimension even though my natural body was still on earth. I knew that Jesus had come to rest upon my spiritual body (one sat on the throne).

Chapter Two

A Different Way of Seeing

Rev 4:3 And he that sat was to look upon like a jasper and a sardine stone: and there was a rainbow round about the throne, in sight like unto an emerald.

Now that we know he has come to sit on our spiritual body, we must keep in mind that God is spirit because he is in a different dimension. It isn't like someone would feel if we sat on them with a lot of weight in one spot. This is just a gentle descending of his Spirit that is perceptible all over our body like a very gentle blanket or a large, soft feather.

When it says "was to look upon" we must remember that we have a new way of seeing just as Helen Keller did. We are feeling something here that is like "a jasper" and we are to use the eyes of our imagination to picture what we are feeling.

The Greek concordance tells us we must go to the Old Testament for a more comprehensive understanding of the word "jasper." In the Hebrew, "jasper" is from a root word meaning "to polish." Webster tells us that "polish" means "rubbing as with a cloth." Keep that in mind as we find our meaning for "sardine stone." The only thing I could find of significance here is that this stone is red. Red signifies God's love because he shed his blood, which is red, for us. The Father gave his only Son to die for us. Jesus was willing to suffer the excruciating pain and humiliation of crucifixion, along with the terrible scourging he endured prior to their nailing his precious hands to the cross because he loves us.

Once the spiritual body is awakened and God's spirit descends on us in a perceptible way, another thing we become aware of is the deep feeling of his love (sardine stone = red) that is like a very gentle massage that is deep inside of our being. It is like a very soft cloth polishing us in very slow, gentle, circular movements such as one would use when gently polishing a precious gem. This feeling is very deep, not on the surface of our skin because it is the spiritual body that is feeling this, and that is inside of our natural body. This is a feeling that never leaves. It is constant. I don't feel it when I'm active such as stacking wood outdoors or vacuuming the carpet indoors, but if I stop for a minute, it is there. This has never left since it began February 11, 1997 when this awesome experience began.

...and there was a rainbow round about the throne, in sight like unto an emerald. From the Greek for round about, this rainbow was not just a half one like we see on earth, but it was a full circle. It was complete. A circle is a symbol of eternal life. It has no beginning and no end. A rainbow is something we see in the sky, a place commonly associated with heaven. Emeralds are green. Green symbolizes life on earth.

I live in western New York where the winters are long and the skies can be gray for several weeks at a time because of the moisture coming from the Great Lakes. The trees look dead and colorless all winter long except for the evergreens that are very dark. One spring my husband and I were returning home after spending a week in Cincinnati where the tulips were blooming and the trees were budding with leaves that were that vibrant shade of green that characterizes the new life of spring. As we drove up the highway on the final leg of our trip home, I couldn't help but notice how gray and dead everything looked. We had another six weeks to go to catch up with the stage of spring we experienced in Cincinnati. In early spring in New York when everything looks dead, I truly long for the fresh green of spring.

When thinking of the rainbow in scripture, the most prominent passage that comes to mind is from Genesis where God made a covenant symbolized by the rainbow that he would never again destroy all flesh by a flood. Putting this all together we have a covenant that not all flesh would be destroyed (rainbow), and that we would have eternal life (circle) and fresh new life on earth (emerald).

With the awakening of the spiritual body and the constant, perceptible touch of God's eternal love, a change begins to take place in our physical body also. There is a new level of vibrant, good health and energy I have experienced in my body since the awakening of my spiritual body. I have no concern that I might contract a life-threatening disease. I will write more about this with a later verse when we find something else around the throne—the four beasts. They will make the message of the rainbow that is in sight like unto an emerald much clearer.

Verse and Interpretation

Rev 4:3 And he that sat was to look upon like a jasper

and a sardine stone: and there was a rainbow round about the throne, in sight like unto an emerald.

I knew that Jesus (he that sat) was making himself known to me through the feeling of his loving presence upon my spiritual body. There was the feeling all over my body of a gentle massage much like one would use when polishing a precious stone (Jasper). The feeling conveyed to me a love deeper than anything I had ever known (sardine stone). This was also the beginning of the preparation of my natural body for putting on immortality (rainbow round about the throne.) New life and vitality were flowing into my natural body (in sight like unto an emerald).

Note: I actually cannot tell the difference between my spiritual body and my natural body. There have been experiences with God and deep studies in other portions of the Bible that have helped me understand the two bodies and how God works in each prior to bringing them together after the sin nature is removed from the natural body. I go into this in greater depth in *The Four Living Creatures*.

* * * * * * * * * * * * * * * * *

Rev 4:4 And round about the throne were four and twenty seats: and upon the seats I saw four and twenty elders sitting, clothed in white raiment; and they had on their heads crowns of gold.

Inserting Keys in Locks

In order to unlock this passage we will need to use some of our previously listed keys. First of all, when decoding encrypted passages, we must view numbers for their spiritual meaning and forget about their numerical value. Twenty-four is 12 times 2. Twelve is the number of governmental perfection. "Twenty-four expresses in a higher form the same signification. It is the number of perfect heavenly government," (Bullinger).

We know that the throne is our spiritual body. The Greek word for "seats" is the exact same word as the word for "throne," so seats are also thrones. However, instead of thrones in the plural, it is singular since 24 is not viewed numerically. There is only one throne, one spiritual body, and it is under perfect, heavenly government. "Round about" means "a circle" and the circle represents eternity or the heavenly realm. Based on all this, my interpretation for the first clause is:

In the heavenly realm, my spiritual body was under perfect heavenly government *(And round about the throne were four and twenty seats)*...

Next clause... *and upon the seats I saw four and twenty elders sitting.* The next word we need to interpret spiritually is "elders." For our spiritual definition of "elders" I turn to the teaching of the early Church Fathers regarding allegory. It has been known for centuries that allegorically men represent certain minds or the understanding; women represent the will. According to this, the elders here in our Revelation passage are a certain mind. Since they are in heaven, they are the spiritual mind. Once again, the number 24 means under perfect heavenly government. The spiritual mind is under perfect heavenly government. So far, my spiritual interpretation of this verse is as follows:

In the heavenly realm, my spiritual body was under perfect heavenly government *(And round about the throne were four and twenty seats)*. And I understood that my spiritual mind was resting upon my spiritual body *(and upon the seats I saw four and twenty elders sitting).*

This spiritual mind was clothed in white raiment. We all know that a mind doesn't literally wear clothes. The white raiment, according to what I read elsewhere in the New Testament speaks of purity of mind and deed, holiness, and overcoming.

The spiritual mind wore crowns. According to the scripture, there are five different crowns promised to those who overcome:

> Incorruptibility – 1 Cor 9:25
> Rejoicing – 1 Thes 2:19
> Righteousness - 2 Tim 4:8
> Life – James 1:12
> Glory – 1 Pet 5:4

I don't intend to quote all these scriptures and elaborate on them, but several have to do with the second coming of Christ. This is exciting because it reinforces in just another way what I'm seeing everywhere in the Scriptures…that this experience is part of the events of the second coming of Christ. He is not just coming in some future event; he is coming right now to those who are ready and looking for him. I truly believe that many who read this book will soon experience similar things to what I am experiencing. Or if you have experienced them this book will give you a deeper understanding of what you are experiencing.

Secrets about the second coming are just everywhere in the Bible, Old and New Testaments, just waiting to be uncovered by those who possess the keys and are willing to take the time to search for them. Each place I study emphasizes a different aspect of the second coming. We need to put them all together to get a more complete understanding.

For greater clarity and ease of understanding my interpretation, I will briefly list here key words from this verse with their spiritual meaning:

- Round about – in a heavenly realm
- Throne – spiritual body
- 24 – perfect heavenly government
- Seats – throne (singular per the spiritual meaning of 24)
- 24 Elders – the spiritual mind under perfect heavenly government
- White raiment – purity, holiness, overcoming
- Crowns--incorruptibility rejoicing, righteousness, life and glory

Verse and Interpretation

Rev 4:4 And round about the throne were four and twenty seats: and upon the seats I saw four and twenty elders sitting, clothed in white raiment; and they had on their heads crowns of gold.

In the heavenly realm, my spiritual body was under perfect heavenly government *(And round about the throne were four and twenty seats)*. And I understood that my spiritual mind was resting upon my spiritual body *(and upon the seats I saw four and twenty elders sitting)*. My spiritual mind had the qualities of holiness, purity, and overcoming. It had also received the promises of Scripture for those who overcome: incorruptibility, rejoicing, righteousness, life and glory *(clothed in white raiment; and they had on their heads crowns of gold)*.

* * * * * * * * * * * * * * * * * * * *

Rev 4:5 And out of the throne proceeded lightnings and thunderings and voices: and there were seven lamps of fire burning before the throne, which are the seven Spirits of God.

This verse holds a most amazing message for the end times. It takes us back to the subject of language I wrote about earlier. We have established that we have a spiritual body and a spiritual mind that are in perfect heavenly government. This means they are free from sin and totally under the authority of Christ who is seated at the right hand of God in heavenly places, "far above all principality, and power, and might, and dominion, and every name that is named, not only in this world, but also in that which is to come" (Eph 1:20, 21).

Our spiritual body and mind are in a place so high and holy that neither Satan nor any of his demons could possibly approach them. From this high and holy place messages are coming forth to the natural part of our being...our natural mind and body. These messages are from God since our spiritual side is perfect and under God's perfect heavenly government. We in our spiritual side have become one with Christ as he himself prayed that we would in John 17. We have that same level of obedience and humility in our spirit as Jesus had when he said, "I only say what I hear the Father say," and "I only do what I see the Father do." Therefore these lightnings, thunderings and voices are heavenly communication coming from Jesus who is also seated with our spirit on our spiritual body. Since Jesus is seated at the right hand of God and one with us resting on our spiritual body, then we are also at the right hand of God.

From this exalted place we are receiving in our natural side communication from God on our spiritual side that is specific and absolutely perfect. We do not hear these messages with our natural ears. We "hear" them as feeling with our newly awakened spiritual body. Here is how it works:

These feelings work in conjunction with our natural mind. I know this because I have been experiencing this kind of communication since February of 1997. Here is one example. A few weeks ago I was in Rochester, NY, where I used to live, grocery shopping. After the clerk scanned the groceries and told me what I owed, I reached into my purse to get my wallet. It was gone! I had no idea where it could be. It all worked out though because my husband who was waiting in the car had money. I called him on my cell phone and soon he was there to pay the bill. I had total peace about the missing wallet which is a new level of trust for me.

Hours later on the way home from Rochester (over an hour's drive) I was wondering about my wallet. I had the thought, "I wonder if it fell out on the floor in my office?" Immediately as I had that thought I felt my face get very warm as though the sun were shining on it. That is a communication from God that I have learned means either "Yes" or "Everything will work out fine." I knew that wallet would be on the floor of my office when I got home. Sure enough, it was.

Sometimes I'll be looking for something in my purse or around my house. (It seems I do that a lot lately!) I'll start to wonder if that item is even in my possession any more. I'll feel that warmth on my face, and I'll know I have the item and if I keep looking, I'll find it. That is true without fail and has happened to me many times.

There are other ways I feel him that may only be communicating his nearness and his love for me. I feel his breath on my right cheek. It is warm, moist and in the rhythm of natural breathing. What comfort to know he is always this close to me. Sometimes I feel a tear on the left side of my face. It is literally wet and salty and I know he is feeling something deeply at the time that communicates something to me. I feel his hand gently brushing the hair away from my face on the left side of my face. It never stops. I have felt the rise and fall of his chest as he breathes close by me. Sometimes I feel his light touch on my hand or arm.

Many times I'll be wondering what I should work on in my daily studies and writings related to the ministries to which God has called me. Should I make a new outline for a new video for the website, work on a website article, work on the book I'm writing, memorize scriptures, etc.? There are many choices for me during those times of study. Often when I get involved in one of these activities, God will touch me in some way to let me know I chose the right direction. However, sometimes I don't take time to ask God and I start doing what I want to do, and that is when the next part of Rev. 4:5 comes into action:

> *...and there were seven lamps of fire burning before the throne, which are the seven Spirits of God.*

Fire has different spiritual meanings in the Bible one of which is purification. Fire purifies and cleanses. The seven Spirits of God refer to the Holy Spirit. Following our key that numbers are only used for spiritual significance in this kind of study, seven means "spiritually perfect." The Holy Spirit is spiritually perfect. Our verse says that these lamps of fire *are* the seven Spirits of God. Therefore, the fire is the Holy Spirit. It is the Holy Spirit who convicts us of sin. This is also a way of hearing that we learn when our spiritual body is awakened. If I have a wrong thought or start to do something God doesn't want me to do, I will experience something unpleasant in my natural body.

I know I'm feeling it in my natural body for at least two reasons: (1) my spiritual body is perfect and therefore doesn't have any unpleasant feelings, and (2) this verse states that the burning lamps of fire are *before* the throne. "Before" also means according to the Greek, "in the presence of." My natural body is in the presence of my spiritual body. This will be made much clearer when we get to the next verse. Here is how this works:

I may start to say something that is prideful or inaccurate and I'll start to cough so much I can't get the words out. A few weeks ago I went out on the porch around 4:00 a.m. to get a couple of logs to throw on the fire. I happened to look up at the sky and noticed all the beautiful stars twinkling in the midst of the totally black sky that we have in the secluded area where we live. It was so lovely that when I went out again for more logs about two hours later I looked up at the sky expecting to see the same thing. However, it was all overcast, and I had the thought, "That figures! That's the way it is when you live in western New York. We don't even get to see the eclipses or meteor showers because it's always cloudy." Immediately my left eye started to itch intensely. I instantly recognized my negative thought and repented.

There have been very strict dealings of God with me regarding diet. One day I reached for the coffee pot to make some coffee for myself. As my hand touched the coffeemaker, I sneezed four times just all of a sudden like out of nowhere. I had wondered if I should drink coffee because I am very sensitive to caffeine. There was my answer…certainly not one I wanted to hear! Black coffee has been my all time favorite beverage, and now I was forbidden to drink it, even decaffeinated. I know, though, that it is for my own good otherwise the Lord would not have forbidden me to have it.

In these ways God directly guides us either through what we are feeling in our spiritual body, which is always good, or through our natural body which is corrective in nature. He is refining us in even the minutest details of our life. The following scripture comes to mind:

> Behold, I will send my messenger, and he shall prepare the way before me: and the Lord, whom ye seek, shall suddenly come to his temple, even the messenger of the covenant, whom ye delight in: behold, he shall come, saith the LORD of hosts. But who may abide the day of his coming? and who shall stand when he appeareth? for he is like a refiner's fire, and like fullers' soap: and he shall sit as a refiner and purifier of silver: and he shall purify the sons of Levi, and purge them as gold and silver, that they may offer unto the LORD an offering in righteousness (Mal 3:1-3).

We are God's temple. The Holy Spirit is preparing us for Jesus to come *in* us. We will judge the world with his righteous judgment, but first we have to be absolutely perfect and pure as gold and silver. When we experience what I have been describing, God will perceptively judge everything even our very thoughts so we have every opportunity to cooperate with him in our coming into holiness.

There is another very important aspect to this new way of experiencing God, and that is we are going to need his perceptible, divine guidance in a very specific way as all hell breaks loose around us. I believe that all sincere Christians will have this experience of the awakening of their spiritual body before this terrible thing happens or right at the time it happens. America is falling to her enemies, and when America falls, the whole world will be affected. I know from the Lord that even now there are foreign troops all over America. They wear civilian clothing and live among us but they are prepared to take us over. They have vast stores of weaponry and instruments of war hidden away in secret places and at some point, they will make themselves known. They will take whatever they want from us, and we will become their slaves. People will be forced out of their homes, families will be separated and all the ravages of war will be forced upon our beloved country. There will be great suffering such as we have never known in America. We have sinned greatly by rejecting and greatly offending our loving Lord who has blessed us with so much. He who has been given much will receive the most severe judgment.

In April of 2009 I had an amazing communication from God such as I have never had before nor since. It came as I was sleeping, but in a sense I wasn't sleeping because this was not like a dream; it was more like a vision. I saw a small tunnel and I was sucked up into it with tremendous force such that it took my breath away and I felt like my stomach dropped to my knees. I was instantly lifted up into the air and found myself looking down on the American countryside. I saw foreign troops running all over the place with rifles in hand taking over everything. Then I was taken through the tunnel again and experienced the same vision once more. "Two" is the number of witness. God was showing me that this is a sure thing. This is truly coming soon. It's interesting that God didn't show me a city being taken over; he showed me the countryside. This makes me think that there is no place safe. Of course they will be in the cities, but those in the country might think they will be spared. Not so.

When this happens we are going to need the Lord desperately. Those who have been truly seeking him, repenting of their sin and allowing him to burn out their dross, will experience him coming to them as I have described. Then they will have this new communication that is certain and sure.

We will face situations such as, for example, running out of food at home and needing to go to a grocery store. In order to get there we will have to pass through enemy checkpoints where our identification will be examined and we will be at their mercy. Can you imagine the terror of facing this? We won't understand their language either because these are foreigners. But if God said to you in the way I have been describing that you should go to the store at 3:30 p.m. Friday, you would know that you would be safe. You wouldn't be guessing about it because his word is certain and you know you can count on it. Our situation will be such that we will not want to move without God's divine guidance.

The Lord has told us that soon we will not get our food from the grocery store but from many different places. Even now we get our milk directly from a farmer. We buy our beef from another farmer who happens to be our neighbor. We go to an Amish community to buy our apples (would you believe $8 for a bushel of apples?) We order several food items online and some of our best friends have big gardens and share their bounty with us.

What I am describing in this experience with God is, I believe, what the parable of the ten virgins is about. The bridegroom is coming. He has come to me in a certain measure, and I expect my experience with him to intensify and branch out into new ways that I don't know about. Christians who have been lazy about their relationship with God will not be able to experience this. One can't mature in Christ quickly. It takes time and experience with God to develop our faith and our character. This is why the foolish virgins can't buy oil. It's not that God would deny them this, but they have rejected him many times such that they have developed calluses over their heart that will take time to remove.

When this happens in America, we will see people all around us who will be desperate for God. They will be holding onto those of us who know him and listening intently to everything we can tell them about him. Every Christian book will become immensely valuable. Those who have longed for revival will see it. Established churches will crumble, and the church will go underground and meet in homes.

When God is speaking to us as I have been describing, we will be able to meet with other believers for worship and Word totally at God's divine direction. There will be severe persecution of the church to the extent that we won't want to communicate verbally or via electronic communications about when and when we will meet. God will sovereignly communicate to each individual and we will all arrive where we are to meet knowing that God directed us and we will be safe.

Verse and Interpretation

Rev 4:5 And out of the throne proceeded lightnings and thunderings and voices: and there were seven lamps of fire burning before the throne, which are the seven Spirits of God.

And out of my spiritual body (out of the throne) came forth messages in various forms that were direct from God (lightening thundering and voices). These messages were to purify everything in me (seven lamps of fire burning) that was in the presence of my spiritual body (before the throne). This work of purification was being done by the Holy Spirit (seven Spirits of God).

Chapter Three

Our Natural and Spiritual Bodies

Rev 4:6 And before the throne there was a sea of glass like unto crystal: and in the midst of the throne, and round about the throne, were four beasts full of eyes before and behind.

The first thing I want to identify here is the four beasts. Once again, "four" is not to be viewed numerically. We are only interested in its spiritual connotation which is "man in relation to the earth as created."

"Beasts," in Greek, is *zoon* pronounced *dzo'-on* meaning "a live thing." My concordance elaborates on this by saying, "All creatures that live on earth, including man are *zoon*." So here we see that both "four" and the definition for "beasts" point to man. This speaks of our natural side, our natural body and mind that relate to things of the earth.

This natural part of us is "in the midst of the throne, and round about the throne." Since the throne is our spiritual body on which rests our spiritual mind, we see that our natural body and mind are very close (in the midst) to the spiritual body and mind and even surround it (round about).

It is important to understand that our spiritual side and our natural side are now very close together as revealed in this verse. When we are immature Christians, we don't know how to access our spirit. We mostly live out of our natural understanding. As we mature in Christ we begin to listen more to our spirit and let it lead us. Since our spirit is united with Christ, as we follow our spirit we are following Christ. Here in this verse we see that these two sides are very close and our natural side is now able to access fully what the spirit that is joined with Christ is communicating. In this way, the natural side is full of eyes before and behind.

Next I will identify the sea of glass that is like unto crystal. The sea of glass is the Bible. The Scripture says that we are to wash ourselves in the water of the Word. A sea is a vast amount of water meaning the entire Bible. It is like glass. You can see through glass. When we reach this stage of our maturation in Christ, we will understand the whole Bible. Passages that we once could not understand will now become clear. This is further shown in the phrase "like unto crystal." The Greek word for "crystal" also means "ice." When water is frozen, it is hard and you can't wash in it. You can't see through it either…at least not very far.

There are portions of the Bible that have been frozen to us. I could not wash myself in Revelation because I did not understand Revelation until now. Once my spiritual body was awakened and I began to experience God in a closer way, I was able to understand many enigmatic portions of Scripture I had never before understood. My spiritual mind was also being awakened and my natural side was coming more under the authority of my spiritual side such that I could see things I had never seen before. This does not mean that I just read a verse and understood it. I have spent many hours studying the Scriptures. This chapter in Revelation opened to me because (1) God told me to study the book in depth, (2) he revealed it to me, and (3) I studied many hours a day using every resource book I could find. However there was still no way I could have understood it before my spiritual body was awakened.

Back to the beginning of this verse, *And before the throne there was a sea of glass like unto crystal,* means that the Bible was in the presence of the spiritual body that had the spiritual mind and Christ resting on it. I have to pick up my Bible and open it and start to read and study. When I do, I am not alone. The Godhead is with me and connected to my natural side is my spiritual body and mind. It took my natural body to pick up the Bible and my natural mind can now understand many things (full of eyes before and behind) because it is being taught by the spiritual part that is inside.

As I study the Word, I can understand passages that I never understood before. I am able to see prophetically (full of eyes before) as the Word shows me things to come. I can understand my past and how it affects my life (behind) as the Word reveals to me either things for which I need to repent or how my life has all come together by God's working in my life.

Verse and Interpretation

Rev 4:6 And before the throne there was a sea of glass like unto crystal: and in the midst of the throne, and round about the throne, were four beasts full of eyes before and behind.

In the presence of my newly awakened spiritual body on which my spiritual mind and Christ were resting *(and before the throne)* the Bible became transparent to me in that I could see down into the depths of the Word as never before *(there was a sea of glass)*. Portions of the Word I had never been able to understand were now opening before me *(like unto crystal)*. Not only did my spirit understand the Word in depth, but my natural mind also understood because it was in close proximity to my spiritual mind.

* * * * * * * * * * * * * * * * * * * *

Rev 4:7 And the first beast was like a lion, and the second beast like a calf, and the third beast had a face as a man, and the fourth beast was like a flying eagle.

This verse reveals what God will be doing with our natural body. Remember there are not four beasts. There is one natural body with which we relate to the natural realm of earth. The spiritual meaning of the numbers and the comparisons to animals will reveal some very exciting things about God's plan for our natural bodies. I'll give you a hint…you won't have to worry about the escalating cost of health insurance anymore!

And the first beast was like a lion… "first" will mean "in the beginning."

One Greek definition for "lion" according to my *Strong's New Expanded Exhaustive Concordance of the Bible* is "figuratively of the imminent peril of death." (This meaning came into being because of so many early Christians being fed to the lions.) So I can say that:

> At first (*And the first*) my natural body *(beast)* was in the imminent peril of death, (*was like a lion*). This has been our condition since the fall; all living things die.

…and the second beast like a calf. "Second" means

"different." Two "is the first number by which we can divide another, and therefore in all its uses we may trace this fundamental idea of *division* or *difference*," (Bullinger). The word "calf" means "anything young." "Young" is defined by Webster as, "fresh, vigorous, strong, lively, and active." My spiritual interpretation of this verse thus far is:

> At first (*And the first*) my natural body *(beast)* was in the imminent peril of death, (*was like a lion*), but it was now different than at first *(and the second beast)* because it was becoming younger. It was fresh, vigorous, strong, lively, and active (*like a calf*).

... and the third beast had a face as a man. "Third" means "divine completeness or perfection" (Bullinger). "A face as a man" will mean "the outward appearance was that of a natural, ordinary person." Adding this to what we already have for this verse:

> At first (*And the first*) my natural body *(beast)* was in the imminent peril of death, (*was like a lion*), but it was now different than at first *(and the second beast)* because it was becoming younger. It was fresh, vigorous, strong, lively, and active (*like a calf*). My body was coming into divine completeness and perfection *(and the third beast*) but yet my outward appearance was that of a natural, ordinary person (*had a face as a man*).

... and the fourth beast was like a flying eagle. "Four" means "man in relation to earth as created." The flying eagle represents rising up and soaring high in a heavenly realm. My final interpretation for this verse now reads:

At first *(And the first)* my natural body *(beast)* was in the imminent peril of death, *(was like a lion)*, but it was now different than at first *(and the second beast)* because it was becoming younger. It was fresh, vigorous, strong, lively, and active *(like a calf)*. My body was coming into divine completeness and perfection *(and the third beast)* but yet my outward appearance was that of a natural, ordinary person *(had a face as a man)*. My natural body on earth *(and the fourth beast)* was rising up into a heavenly realm where death, sickness and aging could no longer affect me *(was like a flying eagle)*.

Now I will restate the verse without the scripture in parentheses:

At first my natural body was in the imminent peril of death, but it was now different than at first because it was becoming younger. It was becoming fresh, vigorous, strong, lively, and active. My body was coming into divine completeness and perfection but yet my outward appearance was that of a natural, ordinary person. My natural body on earth was rising up into a heavenly realm where death, sickness and aging could no longer affect me.

The Bible states that some day *this corruptible must put on incorruption, and this mortal must put on immortality. So when this corruptible shall have put on incorruption, and this mortal shall have put on immortality, then shall be brought to pass the saying that is written, Death is swallowed up in victory. O death, where is thy sting? O grave, where is thy victory?* (1Cor 15:53-55). This is what is happening here in Revelation 4. My corruptible body is putting on incorruption. It began in an instant...one moment I felt as I always had and the next, the awakening had begun in my feet, spread over my entire body and I have never been the same again. It is something the Lord is doing gradually. He may do it instantly in others. It is all according to his will and purpose.

Psalm 103 states that the Lord satisfies our *mouth with good things; so that our youth is renewed like the eagle's.* The Hebrew word for "mouth" here can also be translated "old age" according to *Gesenius' Hebrew-Chaldea Lexicon to the Old Testament.* The Lord satisfies our "old age" with good things so that our youth is renewed like the eagle's.

In our Revelation passage the beast (our natural body) is like a flying eagle. We see the eagle connected with renewed youth in Psalm 103. To me this is a direct and clear confirmation of my interpretation of the "four beasts" being the natural body that is becoming younger. I believe this truly is a promise for the end times. Our youth will be renewed. It starts with the awakening of our spiritual body and we can actually feel God bringing new life into our natural body. There is more about this in greater detail in Daniel 7, which will hopefully be another book, but you might want to start digging there.

Isaiah states, *Even the youths shall faint and be weary, and the young men shall utterly fall, but they that wait upon the LORD shall renew their strength; they shall mount up with wings as eagles; they shall run, and not be weary; and they shall walk, and not faint (Isa 40:30,31).* The Hebrew word for "wait" here means much more than just the passage of time. It means "to bind together." We are being bound together with the Lord as he sits on the throne of our spiritual body. In his close presence with his constant love being felt in our body, the corruption of the curse is being gradually removed from our body. This is along with the eradication of the laws of sin and death which we will see removed in a later chapter in Revelation.

One of my favorite scriptures is from Romans: *But if the Spirit of him that raised up Jesus from the dead dwell in you, he that raised up Christ from the dead shall also quicken your mortal bodies by his Spirit that dwelleth in you (Rom 8:11)*. This says it so plainly…God will quicken our mortal body! He will do it in the same way he raised Jesus from the dead. There is death in our bodies, but God will quicken them. I believe this describes what I feel constantly in my body since Jesus awakened my spiritual body. Very soon, many true believers are going to discover they have a secret room (as God showed my daughter in her dream). There will be great fear and anguish coming upon the people of the world, but at the same time those who are in Christ will feel the awakening of their spiritual body and God's presence with them perpetually.

If you can believe this you should be jumping up and down and shouting "hallelujah" at this point! This word is true. I am experiencing it! I am old enough to qualify for Social Security benefits yet I am healthier and have more energy than at any time in my life. If there were anything wrong with my body I know God would tell me. I have learned any sickness contains a message and serves a purpose to ultimately conform me to his image. When you feel his constant presence in your body with that gentle feeling of floating on a raft on gentle waves along with the constant feeling of being polished by a loving hand, it's hard to believe there could be anything seriously wrong with your body.

I have had numerous dreams that at some point I will become younger. Many years ago I asked God to speak to me in dreams. As he answered that prayer, I wrote them down in journals. I have many journals full of communications from the Lord. I try to notate when he speaks to me in the way I described earlier as feeling the sunshine on my face but sometimes these communications are too numerous to record. I recommend everyone write down what God says to them. It is so helpful sometimes when you are working through something to be able to go back and see what God said years ago.

Having a strong, healthy body does require our participation with God. He has told me to exercise everyday and to use weights. My husband and I walk up the mountain we live on everyday. It is quite a workout. Later I use my weights for a short time.

God has told me not to eat any sugar. He allowed me a few years to adjust to this. At first I could eat one dessert a week but then I stopped even that. He might allow it, I'm not sure, but I just don't want it anymore. I still like ice cream and other sweet things, but I make them myself using stevia and xylitol. These are natural sweeteners that are actually good for you!

His next injunction was to stop eating grains (including rice and corn). I wondered why he said that, but it was very clear. The next day after he said that, I received one of my daily online medical newsletters from Dr. Mercola. He explained that grains turn to sugar after we eat them and that sugar is the main culprit behind cancer, heart disease, diabetes and a host of other serious diseases that Americans are succumbing to by the multiplied thousands. Some of the grains we eat today are different from what grains once were because of many years of man's attempts to "improve" them.

The more I read about nutrition, the more I realize how utterly devoid of nutrition and filled with poisons our food is. Between GMOs and pesticides along with radiation poisoning and who knows what else, there doesn't seem to be much left to eat! The Lord impressed upon me one morning as I was reading my Bible, that if we will pray and ask God to purify our food to our bodies, he will do it. This has become part of our prayer of thanks before we eat each meal. What really matters is doing what God says. I don't eat sugar, grains, or coffee because of God's instructions to me regarding these foods.

When you eat this way, you don't gain weight; in fact, you lose any excess weight you had. You know your immune system is strengthened because you are no longer taking in the sugar that weakens it. Cholesterol levels automatically go where they're supposed to be.

Another benefit of these things the Lord has directed me to do is a further death to my flesh. Also, the Lord instructed me to fast one day a week. I've always hated fasting, but after doing this for a few years, I get along fine with it. When I get up at 2:00 a.m., which I often do, I eat an early supper on fast day!

We Americans are so adverse to discipline and so quick to complain when we don't get everything we want. We are approaching Thanksgiving and my husband and I just reread the account of the first Thanksgiving in Peter Marshall and

David Manuel's book, *The Light and the Glory* which is an historically accurate, thoroughly researched Christian account of the founding of our nation. There was one winter when the Pilgrims survived by eating five kernels of corn a day! This encourages me in my resolve to not complain about anything at all, no matter what. I know God is calling me to this.

Verse and Interpretation

Rev 4:7 And the first beast was like a lion, and the second beast like a calf, and the third beast had a face as a man, and the fourth beast was like a flying eagle.

At first (And the first) my natural body (beast) was in the imminent peril of death, (was like a lion), but it was now different than at first (and the second beast) because it was becoming younger. It was fresh, vigorous, strong, lively, and active (like a calf). My body was coming into divine completeness and perfection (and the third beast) but yet my outward appearance was that of a natural, ordinary person (had a face as a man). My natural body on earth (and the fourth beast) was rising up into a heavenly realm where death, sickness and aging could no longer affect me (was like a flying eagle).

* * * * * * * * * * * * * * * *

This next verse will tell us more about our natural side.

Rev 4:8 And the four beasts had each of them six wings about him; and they were full of eyes within: and they rest not day and night, saying, Holy, holy, holy, Lord God Almighty, which was, and is, and is to come.

By now we know that these are not literal wings spoken of here. They are something that pertains to the natural side of our being because they belong to the beasts. There are six of them so first I'll start with the number "six." Six is the number of man in his imperfection. It is one less than seven which means "spiritual perfection," so this is about something pertaining to our imperfect natural body and mind.

"Wings" are our imagination. Our imagination enables us to fly...to go wherever we want to go in our mind. Once the spiritual body has been awakened and we begin to feel the presence of God continually, we have embarked on a journey into a new land, a heavenly land of new revelations and delights in Jesus, a land free of sickness and weakness. Our imagination becomes more than just an organ of daydreaming or wishful thinking; it becomes our new eyes that enable us to see Jesus and to see ourselves in perfect wholeness with no defects. It is something where God-inspired creativity springs forth and we find ourselves doing things we never dreamed we could do (like write a book!).

Our imagination has the number "six" attached to it. It comes short of perfection and therefore is subject to mistakes or unintentional misuse. God is watching over everything that pertains to our lives such that we can rest in the knowledge that he will guide us in using this imagination. My studies have revealed that the imagination is a part of our mind that is spiritual in nature that became dormant at the fall (see my book, *The Four Living Creatures*). It was not completely dormant but no longer had the capacity Adam and Eve knew in the garden. God wants to awaken our imagination and needs our cooperation to do so. We need to focus these eyes of our heart on learning to envision him and our self with him.

I have written many pages about the imagination in my aforementioned book. It would be good to refer to that book if you have it, or get a copy if you don't. Much of the church has believed for many years that it is wrong to use our imagination because the Bible says in several places in the Old Testament that man's imagination was only evil. An imagination is only evil if the heart is evil. The imagination is a God-created part of our mind. It is the creative part of our mind, and it is into this part of the mind that God speaks from our spirit, the gifts operate and new ideas are birthed

Cultists know that it is with the imagination that the spirit world is accessed. They have also discovered there is power in the imagination, and they use it to curse their enemies and contact demons. Just because evil people use their imagination for evil purposes, we Christians should not shun the imagination altogether. In fact, we really can't. We all imagine things. We imagine what would happen if we lost our job and could no longer pay our bills. We imagine what it would be like if we got cancer or one of our children died in an automobile accident. We can't help but use the imagination because it is part of our mind.

Since we all have an imagination, it seems like a good idea to train it and use it for good things. Actually it is more than a good idea since God is commanding us to use our imagination in these deeper studies. It is everywhere throughout the Scriptures but buried beneath the surface because it is a concept that God reserved for the end times.

Isaiah says, *Thou wilt keep him in perfect peace, whose mind is stayed on thee: because he trusteth in thee* (Isa 26:3).

The Hebrew word for "mind" could just as easily be translated "imagination." Oswald Chambers teaches on this verse in his daily devotional *My Utmost for His Highest* in his entries for February 10 and 11. Some later editions changed the word "imagination" to "mind," but he actually used the word "imagination."

I have ministered several times to hysterical people who were in the midst of a panic attack or some other terrifying experience. Whenever I could get them to imagine Jesus and picture him with them, they calmed down.

The Apostle Paul says ...*we look not at the things which are seen, but at the things which are not seen: for the things which are seen are temporal; but the things which are not seen are eternal* (2 Cor 4:18). The only way I know to do this is with my imagination. I picture Jesus in my mind when I pray. I imagine the New Jerusalem coming down out of heaven. I imagine myself in perfection doing those things God has called me to do.

Jesus used the pictorial language of parables to explain things to his hearers. Today when we read these in Scripture, a picture forms in our mind just as it did in the minds of those who heard him. When I read the parable of the four soils, I get a mental picture of a man sowing seed. I see the newly sprouted seed withering amongst the thorns, and the other seed thriving in good soil, etc.

The imagination takes on new importance with the awakening of our spiritual body because we are able to feel Jesus' touch. He has instructed me, that when I feel his touch, I am to picture him. For example, sometimes when I am sitting quietly, like when I am writing, I feel his gentle hand settling down upon my right shoulder ever so softly. I picture him in my mind and the feeling of his presence intensifies.

Eyes Within

...and they were full of eyes within: The concept of wings being the imagination is reinforced by their having "eyes within." What else could eyes within possibly be but the imagination? Picturing Jesus in our imagination and feeling his touch combine to give us a fuller sense of his presence.

My friend who had the vision of me sitting on the rock in the meadow with Jesus also had other visions for me. I remember one vision where she saw Jesus pouring anointing oil on my head that flowed down over my shoulders. The next day after she had that vision, and for a few days thereafter, I felt that oil coming down over my head onto my shoulders. It was not my physical body that felt it; it was my spiritual body. It was very gentle, but it was unmistakably there. Every few minutes or so, I would feel it slowly flowing down over my head and onto my shoulders. I knew the Lord wanted me to picture this in my mind.

It is very important to develop the eyes of our heart, for in this way we come into a deeper dimension of heaven. Here are a few New Testament scriptures using the word "understanding" *dianoia* in Greek, that could just as easily be translated "imagination" as that is another definition for this Greek word that could have been chosen by the translators.

And we know that the Son of God is come, and hath given us an understanding (dianoia), that we may know him that is true, (1 John 5:20a). God has given us an imagination *(dianoia)* that helps us know him.

In Ephesians 1 Paul prays, *that the God of our Lord Jesus Christ, the Father of glory, may give unto you the spirit of wisdom and revelation in the knowledge of him: the eyes of your understanding being enlightened; that ye may know what is the hope of his calling, and what the riches of the glory of his inheritance in the saints, and what is the exceeding greatness of his power to us-ward who believe, according to the working of his mighty power (Eph1:17-19).*

The "eyes of our understanding" (*dianoia*) could also be translated "the eyes of our imagination." The word "enlightened" (*photizo*) also means "made to see" in Greek. Putting these together, we see that the "eyes of our imagination" need to be "made to see." We receive wisdom and revelation when we stop and envision biblical truth in our imagination thereby taking revelation deeper than just our mind. It goes deep into the heart and connects us to heaven in a perceptible way related to using these newly developed eyes.

In Rev 4:7, our previous verse, we saw that when the spiritual body (throne) is awakened, the physical body (four beasts) begins to rise up into new health and vitality that will cause us to become younger and stronger. We must begin to see our self that way. If we watch television, we are bombarded daily with commercials trying to get us to ask our doctor for various medicines. Pictures of happy people doing what they've always wanted to do because of this medicine are depicted on the screen while the announcer is telling us, as they have to do by law, about all the terrible side effects that may come with this medication. Some of the side effects are far worse than the disease for which the person takes the medicine in the first place. At any rate, we watch these commercials and we hear the announcer saying "When you get cancer, or when you get heart disease, or when you get diabetes, etc." and we begin to believe, based on what we're hearing and the sick people we see all around us, that we are inevitably going to get these diseases as we age. It doesn't have to be that way.

We have got to adjust our thinking and our negative speaking, get obedient to God and rise up out of all this. I'm speaking to myself here as well, as I'm not perfect and I still struggle with some allergy related symptoms I've had my entire life, but I refuse to take on anything else. I don't get alone with God and use my imagination as much as I should even though I know that praying the healing scriptures along with using my imagination on a daily basis does truly bring miraculous healing over time.

Continual Praise

Another aspect of our newly awakened imagination is that of continual praise. This verse says that... *they rest not day and night, saying, Holy, holy, holy, Lord God Almighty, which was, and is, and is to come.* This is very clear and truly needs no interpretation. We are to praise God continually inside our mind. In order to do this, we need to listen to Christian music and sing Christian music. It is helpful to learn the words to the songs, something we can neglect to do if we are looking at the words projected on a screen or in a songbook every time we worship in Church. When I really like a Christian praise song, I listen to it over and over and try to remember the words.

I have to remind myself to listen to Christian music or I'll forget to do it. It's not that I'm listening to something else or don't enjoy praise music, but I am a person who really enjoys silence. Not only do I enjoy silence, but also I need quiet when I am writing or reading a book. Some people do all kinds of reading and writing with music in the background, but for me, it is never in the background and I find it a distraction. When music is playing, I like to give it my attention.

I am aware that I have a praise song going around inside of me continually. Even when I wake up in the night, there is a song there. I don't have to think about it…it is just always there. However, that can be replaced by something else if I haven't been purposefully listening to praise music and happen to hear the wrong music…it could even be a commercial. If I realize I've lost that praise music, I make sure to listen to some to ensure that I get it back.

The imagination is an amazing thing. In my imagination I can hear Sandi Patty and Larnelle Harris singing "I've Just Seen Jesus," or Selah singing "Glory," a couple of my favorites. I believe, and my studies reveal, that if I will diligently purpose to use my imagination to worship Jesus, I will be able to hear the music of heaven some day. As I said before, this faculty of our mind is something that was greatly reduced as a result of the fall, and God is working with us to restore it today, but it requires our cooperation and discipline along with holiness to achieve this.

Verse and Interpretation

Rev 4:8 And the four beasts had each of them six wings about him; and they were full of eyes within: and they rest not day and night, saying, Holy, holy, holy, Lord God Almighty, which was, and is, and is to come.

And the natural body (four beasts) had an imagination

(six wings). This imagination had no limitations (full of eyes). It was able to praise God continually (rest not day and night). It knew that God was, always had been and always would be eternal God and holy in all his character and actions.

* * * * * * * * * * * * * * * * *

Rev 4:9-11 And when those beasts give glory and honor and thanks to him that sat on the throne, who liveth for ever and ever, the four and twenty elders fall down before him that sat on the throne, and worship him that liveth for ever and ever, and cast their crowns before the throne, saying, "Thou art worthy, O Lord, to receive glory and honor and power: for thou hast created all things, and for thy pleasure they are and were created."

Before I continue with the interpretation of these verses, it would be helpful to review what I have shown thus far:

- Beasts – our natural body and mind
- Throne – our newly awakened spiritual body
- God – One who rests upon our spiritual body
- 24 elders – our spiritual mind under the perfect, heavenly government of God
- Crowns – all the good qualities and blessings we have because of God

These last few verses show what happens in the spirit realm when we praise God on earth. Based on our previous verse, we know that this praise should continually be going around in our imagination and that we are to purposely listen to and learn worship songs to ensure that this does happen. When we do this, God, who is seated on our spiritual body, hears this praise. We do not need to sing the songs out loud for him to hear them because he is within us resting on our spiritual body. We do not have to consciously think about this praise, because as long as we have listened to praise or participated in it on a regular basis, these songs automatically go around inside us. However, it is good to purposely sing praise to God in your mind. This is something you can do anywhere at any time.

Many times I have been aware that a song I had not thought of for many years was going around inside my mind. When I recognize this and think about the words, it is often a message from God. One time many years ago we were in dire financial need. We had faithfully tithed and served God in ministry for many years, but we had finally come to the point where, not because of any debt or foolish spending, we could not pay our electric bill. I went to bed one night heavily burdened over our financial situation. I had only slept a short time, when I awoke with a song in my mind. The words to the song were, "I know everything's gonna' be all right." I knew I had heard from God and was able to find peace. God did some amazing things to bring us out of our situation, including taking us to a new level of humility.

According to these last verses of Revelation 4, I can see that when I worship God in my natural, conscious mind that dwells in my natural body (beasts) which is something I can do perpetually in my imagination, then my spiritual mind also worships God in total submission (24 elders falling down before him in worship). I believe that this total submission of the spiritual mind connected to my natural side's worship in the natural realm, makes it possible for God to supernaturally direct every aspect of my life.

For example, my husband and I are continually amazed at the way God has us in the right place at the right time and gives us many "divine appointments" with other people. We spend several hours a week driving our car on curvy, mountainous country roads. There are always dead deer at the side of the road. We know several people personally who have hit one. Many times deer cross just ahead of us or just behind us. Every time we drive away from our home, we pray God's protection over our home, our travel and specifically that we will not hit a deer or other large animal. We know that God directs our comings and our goings and watches over us as we remain submitted to him. This will be extremely important in the days ahead as our nation is occupied by foreign troops. Great peace and comfort will come as we remain continually in God's presence submitted under his divine guidance through worship.

This heavenly worship also shows us a picture of humility. In this state of perpetual worship, our spiritual side is continually giving God all the praise and glory for every good thing in our lives. Pride is perhaps our greatest enemy. We will find safety and peace in humility which is perhaps the greatest of all virtues.

Our spiritual side is still behind a veil. Continual praise keeps the veil open so that communication can flow from side to side. As we continue through our study of Revelation in future books, we will see that the veil is going to disappear and we will have direct access to heaven and see Jesus face to face.

Verse and Interpretation

Rev 4:9-11 And when those beasts give glory and honor and thanks to him that sat on the throne, who liveth for ever and ever, the four and twenty elders fall down before him that sat on the throne, and worship him that liveth for ever and ever, and cast their crowns before the throne, saying, "Thou art worthy, O Lord, to receive glory and honor and power: for thou hast created all things, and for thy pleasure they are and were created."

When I worship God in my natural, conscious mind that dwells in my natural body (beasts) which is something I can do perpetually in my imagination, then my spiritual mind (twenty-four elders) also worships God in total submission (falling down before him in worship).

* *

I hope this chapter has been an encouragement to you. The Lord told us in 1972 that he was going to shake everything that could be shaken and nothing would be left standing that was not rooted and grounded in him. We are literally seeing this take place on a daily basis. Every trusted institution in this nation and other nations in the world are falling. Our government and our economy are not based in God. They will also fall and are, in fact, in that very process even now. May we all take hope in knowing that our Lord is very near. He who spoke into existence the world and everything in it will provide for our every need if we remain faithful to him.

Chapter Four

Who Is on the Throne?

Rev 5:1 And I saw in the right hand of him that sat on the throne a book written within and on the backside, sealed with seven seals.

In Revelation Four a new door is opened into the spiritual realm of heaven. Once again we see a throne and the one sitting on the throne is holding a book in his hand. First we will identity what the book represents and then we will talk more about who is on the throne. As always in my revelatory end-time teachings, the scriptural passage is to be viewed as inward and allegorical rather than outward and literal. The book of Revelation will only be understood correctly if viewed allegorically.

The Greek word for book used here is *biblion*. It is defined as a small book. It can also be "a sheet on which something has been written" (Thayers). That reminds me of another Greek word that means "something on which something is written." That word is epistle or *epistole* in Greek which means "a written message." So we can see that a book and an epistle are close to being the same thing.

In Scripture an epistle can represent our heart. In 2 Corinthians 3 Paul speaks of believers as being epistles, or what we would call today, letters. These were written on their hearts.

Do we begin again to commend ourselves? or need we, as some others, epistles of commendation to you, or letters of commendation from you? Ye are our epistle written in our hearts, known and read of all men: Forasmuch as ye are manifestly declared to be the epistle of Christ ministered by us, written not with ink, but with the Spirit of the living God; not in tables of stone, but in fleshly tables of the heart (1 Cor 3:1-3).

If a book and an epistle are alike, and if an epistle can represent our heart as Scriptures states, then a little book can also represent our heart. That is what I'm seeing here in Rev 5. This one on the throne is holding in his right hand, the hand of power, the heart of a believer. When we continue our study of the seven seals that are on this book, a study encompassing several verses and other chapters, we will see that this interpretation consistently appears to be quite accurate.

At this point it would be good to clarify what our heart actually is. First we will look at both the Greek and Hebrew words for heart. In the Greek, the word for heart is *kardia* which means "the thoughts, the mind and (by analogy) the middle." Of course, it is from this word we get our words for things related to our heart such as cardiac, cardiology, etc. The heart is the most important organ in our natural body. Also regarding our inner life, our heart is most important because it is our mind, the center of our thoughts and feelings.

In the Old Testament the word for heart is *labe*. There it is defined as being "the thoughts, the feelings, the will, and (by analogy) the middle." The heart is so central to our being, so important, that it came to stand for all of humankind's mental and moral activity.

As we read the first verse of Revelation 5, we see that the book is sealed with seven seals. We have established that the book is our heart, so here we see that our heart is sealed to us in many ways. Actually we don't really know our own heart. Jeremiah says that the heart of humankind is "deceitful above all things and desperately wicked." Then he asks the question, "Who can know it?" The fact is we can't know our own heart and no other human being can know our heart. However the next verse in Jeremiahs states, "I the LORD search the heart, I try the reins, even to give every man according to his ways, and according to the fruit of his doings" (Jer 17:10). We can find comfort in knowing that Jesus knows our heart and in these end times, he will be revealing to us what is in our heart. There are many things lodged deep in our heart that must be exposed and thoroughly dealt with if we are to come into the fullness of Christ in these end times. In the ensuing chapters of Revelation God will show us what is in our heart as each seal is removed.

This book, our heart, is written within and on the backside. What is within stands for who we are based on all the decisions we have made in our life. The backside represents all the things that ever happened to us in the past. Who we are on the inside is rooted in the things that happened to us in the past, the backside. Many of these things in our past were misunderstood by us and in our ignorance we made decisions and formed beliefs that were sinful and unbelieving. Most of these events and our responses to them are no longer remembered by us, but Jesus can bring them to our remembrance and help us clear out the lies, unforgiveness and other things still lodged there that, although we are not aware of them, can still affect our life. We cannot change our past, but we can change our response to the events of the past regarding what happened in our heart at the time. We can only do this if Jesus reveals to us what is in our heart.

This book has seven seals. Of course, there are not literally seven seals on our heart. Seven is a number which symbolically means spiritual perfection. This is God's plan and intention for our lives, that we become perfect even as Jesus himself is perfect. As long as our heart is sealed, we won't be able to come into this perfection, but Jesus will bring us to this state of purity by perfectly revealing what is in our heart. He is the only one who can do this.

It is as Jesus reveals what is in our heart that we gradually come into spiritual perfection. This is according to God's will. It is God's plan and purpose that we not be able to see into our own heart. If we were able to do so, we would feel we did not need God as much and we might try to deal with things in our heart that we're not ready to deal with. So it is God himself who shows us what is in our heart.

We need to draw apart from the busyness of everyday life and spend quiet time with the Lord. It is at these times we can talk over with him situations in our life, things about ourselves we want to change, seek his guidance, etc. As we seek him, he will begin to show us things in our heart that only he knows. He will give us specific information that we can work through with his help. In this way our relationship with God develops as we gradually come into spiritual perfection as he reveals our heart to us. And as we come to know what is in our heart and to be cleansed of things that should not be there, we come to know God in a much fuller way. So only God can show us what it is our own heart as well as how our past has affected us.

Now that we have established that the book is our heart, we need to determine who is sitting on the throne holding our heart. In Revelation 4 John sees someone sitting on a throne whose description sounds very much like God. This puzzled me for years as I wondered why God would be holding my heart in his hand to give to Jesus. After all Jesus is God. Does God give my heart to God? To be more specific, does Father God have my heart in his right hand to give to the Lamb, Jesus? I thought it was Jesus who worked in us to present us to his Father. It just didn't make sense. Then I realized that when John saw Jesus on the throne in Revelation 4, it states that John was "in the spirit." A door had opened before him and he was "in the spirit." Maybe he could only see Jesus on the throne when he was "in the spirit." Let me explain the throne and then all this will make sense.

I explained in Revelation 4 what the throne is. (I will give a more thorough explanation of the throne at the end of this chapter.) We are the throne Jesus rests upon. More specifically, it is the spirit side of our being that is the throne Jesus rests upon. Now here is my revelation: When we are in the spirit (as John was in Revelation 4), Jesus is on the throne of our life. When we are in the flesh, we are on the throne of our life. The one on the throne is the one who has authority and makes the decisions. If I get in the flesh, I'm the one doing that and I'm the one on the throne at that time. This is why the book is in the right hand of the one on the throne. The right hand is scripturally defined (O.T.) as the hand of power and direction. (In the Hebrew language, the definitions for right hand and left hand are quite different.) In the Greek, the word for right hand used here is *dexios*, and is defined as "the hand that usually takes." This definition describes what happens when we sit on the throne of our life rather than Jesus. We have taken that position from him and we have the book (heart) in our own hand.

The book has seven seals that are opened in some of the remaining chapters of Revelation. If you know your Bible you will remember that the first four seals are the four horses and their riders described in Rev 6. How can these be in our heart? If viewed outwardly they obviously cannot be, but when seen allegorically, they definitely can be and are in our heart.

Now that we have identified the book, the throne and the person on the throne we can put together a concise interpretation for Rev 5:1:

Verse and Interpretation

Rev 5:1 And I saw in the right hand of him that sat on the throne a book written within and on the backside, sealed with seven seals.

I realized (saw) that I was trying to direct my own life by making decisions on my own rather than allowing Jesus to control my life (right hand of him who sat on the throne). I was trying to control my mind, my thoughts and my emotions (book in own hand) but I did not understand myself (written within) or my past (backside) as all the things I needed to understand about myself were unknown to me (sealed with seven seals).

The Throne

Before continuing on to the next verse, there are a few more things I would like to say about the throne and why it represents the spiritual side of our being. First of all, this does not necessarily mean that every scripture in the whole Bible where throne is mentioned (and throne appears 165 times) is speaking of our spiritual being. Sometimes it is referencing something else according to the context, but there are enough places where throne is given a human attribute that lead me to believe it is our life allegorically in Revelation. For example:

- A woman blesses the king by saying "…the king and his throne be guiltless" (2 Sam 14:9).
- The Lord has "…prepared his throne for judgment" (Psa 9:7). Are we not the ones God is preparing for judgment since we are to judge the world? (1 Cor 6:2)
- "…God sitteth upon the throne of his holiness" (Psa 47:8). Can a piece of furniture be holy?
- "When the Son of man shall come in his glory, and all the holy angels with him, then shall he sit upon the throne of his glory" (Matt 25:31). I believe the church is the throne of his glory that he will sit upon. He will be in us judging the world when we, his body, are joined with him, the head, at the second coming.

Solomon's throne is described in detail in 1 Kings and 2 Chronicles. There must be a good reason for the Lord putting this information in our Bible. Let's look at these passages now and see how they metaphorically might represent a person. First we'll look at 1 Kings:

Moreover the king made a great throne of ivory, and overlaid it with the best gold. The throne had six steps, and the top of the throne was round behind: and there were stays on either side on the place of the seat, and two lions stood beside the stays. And twelve lions stood there on the one side and on the other upon the six steps: there was not the like made in any kingdom (1 Kings 10 18-20).

The throne was made of ivory which speaks of the purity (white) of the natural man (ivory comes from an animal, something natural). It is overlaid with gold which metaphorically speaks of God because of its value and purity. So thinking of this as a person, we see this person has a life of purity and has put on Christ.

Another indication this pertains to a person is the number six. Six is the number of man, man having been created on the sixth day. The word "steps" in Hebrew is interesting because it is defined as, "elevation; a journey to a higher place" (Strong's 4609). So we see that this person has a life of purity (ivory) and has put on Christ (gold) by way of a spiritual journey (six steps) that elevated him/her spiritually to the seat of the throne, which I will explain shortly.

The Top

"…and the top of the throne was round behind:"

This throne has certain characteristics of a human body that will be revealed as we look at the meanings of the Hebrew words used here. The first body part seen here is the head which is found in the word "top." "Top" in Hebrew means head. This head is round. Round means in Hebrew "to revolve." Isn't that exactly what our head does when we are seated? While our body remains stationary, our head moves left and right and up and down. It revolves.

Behind

This word "behind" actually means behind; so how does that fit in here? Why is the head behind? Our spiritual body is behind our natural body. I stated earlier that the throne is the spiritual side of our being. To be more specific, it is our spiritual body. Just as my natural body has a head at the top, so does my spiritual body. You cannot see the spiritual body but everyone has one. When this natural body dies, the spiritual body, which looks just like it, is released into the spiritual world. In these end times, God will be awakening and maturing our spiritual body as part of the process of bringing us into the fullness of Christ with a fully redeemed body.

Stays

"...there were stays on either side..." The Hebrew word for stays is *yad* and it is most often translated as "hand." It is translated "hand" 1,359 times. The next usage of *yad* is the word "by" used only 44 times.

We can see that *yad* is definitely the word for hand throughout the whole Old Testament. So very clearly we see here that this throne, this person, has hands. The hands are on either side of the seat. So what is the seat?

Seat

The Hebrew word for "seat" is *shebeth*, which can also be translated as "abode" or "dwelling." This is the trunk of the body where our true dwelling place is in our heart, the most important organ of the body. We don't think of our self as being in our hand or any other appendage of the body. We feel our self as being in the trunk of our body and in our heart, the seat of our emotions.

Footstool

We cannot have a body without feet. These are notated in the description of the throne found in 2 Chronicles 9:18:

> The throne had six steps, and a footstool of gold was attached to it (NIV)

The word footstool is mentioned seven times in the Old Testament. Every place but here it is comprised of two Hebrew words, one meaning stool and the other meaning foot. But a different word is used here in 2 Chronicles and this is the only time it is used in the whole Bible. It is *kebesh* and is defined as "a footstool (as trodden upon)." We tread upon the ground, or the floor, with our feet. It even says that this footstool was attached to the throne. This is the only place in Scripture where a footstool is attached to anything. This is a clear indication to me that the footstool mentioned here was clearly to be viewed as an allegorical type of our feet.

So there you have it—a description of a throne that is clearly describing a human body when looking at word definitions, usages, and allegory as identified by Scripture. This body is pure (ivory,) covered with Christ (gold,) has a head (top) and hands (stays), a trunk (seat) and feet (footstool). The six steps also indicate this is a person as six is the number of humankind. This is a spiritual body as indicated by it being behind.

Chapter Five

Who Can Know My Heart?

Rev 5:2 And I saw a strong angel proclaiming with a loud voice, Who is worthy to open the book, and to loose the seals thereof?

In Scripture, angels are defined in both Greek and Hebrew as messengers. They can also be any of the following "a prophet, priest, teacher, pastor, ambassador, or king." From this definition we can see that angels can also be people. Usually we think of an angel as being a supernatural messenger from God. I have never seen nor heard what I would consider to be an angel as we think of them, but I have had supernatural messages from God delivered to me through his ministering agents on earth particularly his prophets. Sometimes experiences in life are God's messengers. When something of an adverse nature happens to us over and over again, this experience may be a way of God telling us that something is in our own heart that needs to be dealt with.

I had something like this in my own life. It seemed that I just could not get ahead in a certain area of my life. I felt like I was getting shot down over and over again. It was like running into a brick wall. As I continually sought God as to why I had this, he revealed to me a belief deep in my heart that had been there since I was a little child—something I had judged him wrongly about. Because that judgment was lodged in my heart, God could not bless me in certain ways. Once he revealed it to me and I repented of it, my life changed and I never had that problem again. However, I had no way of knowing what was in my heart. I had to seek God for that, and once he revealed that to me I was able to get free from it.

It says in Proverbs 4:23, "Keep thy heart with all diligence; for out of it are the issues of life." That word "keep" is sometimes translated "guard." Our life is determined by what is in our heart, therefore we need to guard our heart and be very careful about what is in our heart. We need to be quick to forgive and slow to judge other people. We should be careful what we see with our eyes and what we take in through our ears. We want to guard our heart and be sure we are obeying God in everything we possibly can. In order to do this we need to stay in his Word and let the Holy Spirit judge our lives daily according to his Word. Our ears need to be open to hear these spiritual messages God has for us.

This verse states that he *saw* a strong angel. To see, *eido* in Greek, also means to know or understand. It is the same verb used in 1 John 2:4: " He that saith, I know *(eido)* him, and keepeth not his commandments, is a liar..." This is not speaking of actually seeing Christ but of knowing him in relationship. So here in Rev 5:2 he is not actually seeing an angel but he is beginning to understand a strong message in life (strong angel). Now we can say that this person who has taken control of his own life (the one on the throne with his heart in his own hands) is beginning to understand (saw) through a difficult experience in life (strong angel) that he needs to know why this difficult experience has occurred.

He has finally realized that blaming everyone else around him for his dire circumstances is not going to help because the problem is in his own heart. This is a vital step necessary for moving forward into full maturity in Christ. We must come to the realization that our circumstances in life are there because we need these circumstances to show us what is in our own heart. For example, if someone goes through life being rejected over and over again by his peers, it is because in his own heart he expects to be rejected. He believes people will reject him and because of this expectation in his own heart, he unconsciously does things or projects in some way this expectation such that others perceive it and react to it. Eventually he comes to a realization (he sees or knows) through experiences in life (strong angel) that something in his own heart (the book) is causing these experiences and someone needs to tell him what it is in his heart that causes these things.

Verse and Interpretation

Rev 5:2 And I saw a strong angel proclaiming with a loud voice, Who is worthy to open the book, and to loose the seals thereof?

And I understood (saw) from a difficult experience in my life (angel proclaiming in a loud voice) that someone needed to show me what was in my own heart (who is worthy to open the book) and reveal to me those things that I could not discover on my own (loose the seals thereof).

* *

Rev 5:3 And no man in heaven, nor in earth, neither under the earth, was able to open the book, neither to look thereon.

Usually when we encounter difficulties in life that don't just go away on their own, we start looking for help. We might enquire of our friends and ask their help. Perhaps we go a step further and seek out a counselor or a minister who can help us. Self-help books are available on any subject imaginable, and of course, there is always the Internet with a myriad of websites on any subject that interests us. If we want to know how to do something to solve our problem, all we have to do is go to YouTube and someone will have a video on how to do it!

People may go to hypnotists hoping they can solve their problem. They often go to psychiatrists and get medication for their problem. Some try seeking help from a deceased relative by going to a séance. There is no end to the things people may do to find help but all to no avail. They might find a brief respite from their problem but it always returns. They may realize the problem is within, but they don't know how to discover what it is so they can fix it. A wise person will know that only Jesus can fix what is in their heart but we often don't seriously seek his help until we have exhausted all other possible resources.

It is part of our sin nature to want to control our own life. We want to be strong and independent thinking this is a sign of maturity when actually maturity in Christ only comes when we realize our own inadequacy to manage life on our own. God wants us to seek him for everything in our life right down to the smallest details. He cares about everything we do and think and in his great love for us wants us to include him in all aspects of our daily living. Most sincere Christians will pray every day in their devotional time but then quite often go about the rest of their day without including him in other things. He wants so much more. It takes a difficulty (strong angel) such as this person on the throne of his life has encountered to bring us to the place where we realize how desperately we need Jesus.

Verse and Interpretation

Rev 5:3 And no man in heaven, nor in earth, neither under the earth, was able to open the book, neither to look thereon.

And I realized there was no one in heaven nor in earth neither under the earth who was able to open my heart and see what was there.

* * * * * * * * * * * * * * * *

Rev 5:4 And I wept much, because no man was found worthy to open and to read the book, neither to look thereon.

After exhausting all possible resources for discovering what is in his heart, this person has come to the end of himself. To weep much, *klaio* in Greek, means to wail aloud. Now he knows there is no way of finding out what he so desperately wants to know about himself. Absolutely no one can help him. He has come to the end of his own fleshly attempts and has given up. This is exactly where the Lord wants each of us to be so he can finally complete the work in our heart that can only be done by him. So long as we are seeking to do it in our own strength, the Lord just waits. It is imperative that we come to this place of desperation and failure so the Lord can begin his way of revealing our heart to us and working in us.

Verse and Interpretation

Rev 5:4 And I wept much, because no man was found worthy to open and to read the book, neither to look thereon.

And I wept much because no one was found worthy to know what was in my heart.

* * * * * * * * * * * * * *

Rev 5:5 And one of the elders saith unto me, Weep not: behold, the Lion of the tribe of Judah, the Root of David, hath prevailed to open the book, and to loose the seven seals thereof.

A Review of the Elders

Finally, out of his desperation, this person is able to hear a word of encouragement. It is from "one of the elders." We know that Revelation speaks of 24 elders being seated around the throne of God. I suppose this could be taken literally, but I believe the 24 elders are just as symbolic as a lamb with seven horns and seven eyes. Men, according to the early Church Fathers, represent certain minds or the understanding. Therefore, the elders represent something about our mind and our understanding.

The number 24 will reveal more. When deciphering heavily encrypted scripture passages, numbers should be treated only for their spiritual meaning not the numerical. To view them numerically blocks the revelation. Twenty-four is two times twelve. Twelve is the number of perfection of government; twenty-four is a higher form of the same signification and is therefore the perfection of divine government in heaven. (Bullinger)

When we put together (1) the allegorical type of men as certain minds or the understanding with (2) perfection of divine government in heaven, we can now ascertain that the 24 elders represent our spiritual mind. It is our spiritual mind that understands spiritual things. The 24 elders are often seen worshiping God. That is also a function of our spiritual mind.

Now that we understand the twenty-four elders represent our spiritual mind, we can conclude that this person who is weeping because he does not know what is in his own heart and has ceased searching for help apart from Jesus has finally quieted himself enough that he can hear what the Lord is saying to him through his spiritual mind. It is our spiritual mind that is in union with the mind of Christ and therefore able to hear his messages to our natural mind. The message is that Jesus is the one who has gained the victory for him. He is the one who can open his heart and reveal to him the things he needs to know in order to overcome, with God's help, those things locked up in his heart.

Verse and Interpretation

Rev 5:5 And one of the elders saith unto me, Weep not: behold, the Lion of the tribe of Juda, the Root of David, hath prevailed to open the book, and to loose the seven seals thereof.

My spiritual mind caused me to understand (one of the elders) that Jesus (the Lion of the tribe of Judah, the Root of David), was able to disclose to me what was in my heart (prevailed to open the book) and set me free (loose the seven seals) from all that was therein (thereof).

* * * * * * * * * * * * * * * * * * * *

Rev 5:6 And I beheld, and, lo, in the midst of the throne and of the four beasts, and in the midst of the elders, stood a Lamb as it had been slain, having seven horns and seven eyes, which are the seven Spirits of God sent forth into all the earth.

In this verse he has a greater revelation of who Jesus is and where Jesus is. In the midst of all this symbology we are shown the omnipresence of God, his omnipotence and his omniscience.

His omnipotence is expressed as seven horns. Horns represent power throughout the Bible. The number seven means spiritual perfection and completeness. Putting together horns and seven we can interpret this as power (horns) that is spiritually perfect and complete (seven).

His omniscience is shown in type as being seven eyes. Certainly it is with our eyes that we see and therefore know. As God, his ability to see and know all things is spiritually perfect and complete (seven).

His omnipresence is a little more difficult to see in this verse until we identify what is represented by the four beasts. It was necessary for God to use symbology here because at this point and beyond in Rev 5 the Holy Spirit will reveal to us the information that was to be known only by the church of the end times. We are the only ones who will be able to understand this because we will experience it. I have already experienced some of this and because of this I can see it in the Word. Had I not had this experience with God, I could not possibly understand this. I described my experience in Revelation 4 and will repeat it in Rev 5:8 a little further on in this book.

The interpretation of the four beasts is amazing and so far removed from the way it has always been understood that, even though I explained this in my interpretation of Revelation 4, I will repeat it here. The Greek word interpreted as "beasts" here is different from the word for "beasts" used in regards to the beast associated with the dragon and the false prophet. For the four beasts the Greek word for beast is *zoon* which means "a live thing, i.e. an animal." The word for beast used in regards to the beast that is named with the dragon and the false prophet is *therion* meaning "a dangerous animal, a venomous, wild animal." *Therion* is also used for the beast that rises up out of the sea having seven heads and ten horns in Rev 13. So the four beasts is a term used for a live thing, an animal.

When interpreting Scripture symbolically we will never discern the Holy Spirit's message if we take numbers literally. In other words, they are not to be understood numerically but only spiritually. Part of keeping the message secret has been by use of numbers. Numbers also will reveal the true message to us if we understand them spiritually according to the way they are consistently used throughout the Bible. E. W. Bullinger in his book *Number in Scripture* devotes twelve pages to the number four alone where he traces its usage throughout the entire Bible. He states, "Four is emphatically the number associated with the creation of earth and of man in relation to earth as created." With this in mind, we must understand that there are not literally "four" beasts, or as some other translations say, four living creatures. They have something to do with earth and human beings.

Putting together the Greek word for beast, *zoon*, "a live thing, i.e. an animal" and the number four, "man in relation to earth as created," we can see that the four beasts are definitely concerning something of earth, more specifically an animal, but not just any animal. This is "man" or to be more inclusive we can say "humankind." This is the animal part of us. It represents our physical body.

Let's look at Rev 5:6 again: "And I beheld, and, lo, in the midst of the throne and of the four beasts, and in the midst of the elders, stood a Lamb as it had been slain, having seven horns and seven eyes, which are the seven Spirits of God sent forth into all the earth." This is presented as though it is something we are looking at that is outside of ourselves, but that is not the case. This is within. To interpret it as outward keeps the mystery unsolved. To view it as inward is a major key for finding the true interpretation.

With this view and what I have identified so far, we can now see that what this person in Rev 5 is seeing is within himself. He understands that Jesus is within him. When we go through trials as this person was experiencing, we might even feel that Jesus is far away, that he doesn't know what we are experiencing or that he doesn't care. This person now knows this is not the case. He sees that within himself, in the midst of his spiritual body (throne), his physical body (four beasts), and his spiritual mind (the elders), there is Jesus in his omnipotence(seven horns) and his omniscience (seven eyes). When we understand this, we begin to see how very close and personal Jesus is (his omnipresence). He is not far away in heaven somewhere, he is in heaven within us, and heaven is a spiritual realm that we will be entering fully in the end times even though we are still on the earth living in a physical body. It is within us but it has been closed to us. It has been kept behind a veil where we were not aware of it.

Heaven is very real and very vast and we enter it from within but only as we become purified such that we are like Jesus in our character. This is a process that true believers will go through in these end times that will bring us into the fullness of Christ and therefore in him we will have access to heaven. As we learn more about Revelation we will see that this process of becoming holy and totally pure is something that God will lead us into. He does the work in us but we must cooperate with him and obey him totally. There will be a new awareness that Jesus is with us and that he speaks to us often and in many ways. This will be a communication that has not been granted to believers of past ages. This communication will make it possible for God to speak to us about every little detail of our lives and in this way we will come into perfection as we cooperate with him. God reveals, we obey, and God does the work, a work that will transform us such that "this mortal will put on immortality."

We are going to have to come to this place if we are to survive the destruction of our entire planet that is now in full force but still hidden from the eyes of the masses. Those who get their news from the mainstream media are mostly getting propaganda and lies, not truth. To know what is really happening in our world we must turn to the alternative news on the Internet…and even there we must use discernment.

I will give just one example of many truths that are being withheld. The Japan earthquake and resultant tsunami that destroyed the Fukushima nuclear plant in March 2011 was a disaster beyond biblical proportions. As of the writing of this book, March 2016, the Fukushima nuclear plant has never stopped spewing enormous amounts of radioactive water and materials into the Pacific Ocean and no one knows how to stop it. There are grave concerns that almost all life in the Pacific Ocean is dying rapidly. The radiation has spread across the ocean to the west coast of North America and from there across the entire continent. We are not being told. In fact, San Diego has built a billion-dollar desalinization plant so that in spite of the drought, the city will have water. No one is telling them that the water will be radioactive. Even the ground water in the western United States is becoming radioactive.

Practically no one tells the public that the animals and fish are dying of radiation poisoning everywhere along our west coast. I recently read an article on the AccuWeather site about the fact that thirty whales have beached in Alaska and scientists don't know why they are dying. I suspect they know but are not permitted to speak of it. I even read that anyone taking a Geiger counter to the beach to check radiation levels will be arrested. There is so much I could write about this, but that is not the purpose of this book. I only give this one illustration to point out that we must be changed if we are to live on this planet. If our oceans die, we die. This is happening now. It is only a matter of time until the Atlantic Ocean is also polluted with radiation. This radiation will be around for thousands of years. There will be no life on earth unless God does something miraculous. If we ever doubted that we are living in the end times, this one illustration should prove beyond a doubt that this is true. The radiation is actually changing the human genome and this damage is irreparable.

Returning to Rev 5:6 there is one more thing that needs to be identified. This is the Seven Spirits of God sent forth into all the earth. This represents the Holy Spirit. "Seven" means spiritually perfect and complete as opposed to a literal rendering of seven spirits. Jesus said:

> And I will pray the Father, and he shall give you another Comforter, that he may abide with you forever; Even the Spirit of truth; whom the world cannot receive, because it seeth him not, neither knoweth him: but ye know him; for he dwelleth with you, and shall be in you. I will not leave you comfortless: I will come to you (John 14:16-18).

It is easy to see in this passage that Jesus is telling them that he will come to them as the Comforter. Jesus is the Comforter. We see this in the latter part of Rev 5:6: "stood a Lamb as it had been slain, having seven horns and seven eyes, which are the seven Spirits of God sent forth into all the earth." The Lamb with the seven horns and seven eyes is the seven Spirits of God. We see here that within this person is Jesus (Lamb) and the Holy Spirit (seven Spirits of God). The Father is also there because Jesus said, "At that day ye shall know that I am in my Father, and ye in me, and I in you" (John 14:20).

Verse and Interpretation

Rev 5:6 And I beheld, and, lo, in the midst of the throne and of the four beasts, and in the midst of the elders, stood a Lamb as it had been slain, having seven horns and seven eyes, which are the seven Spirits of God sent forth into all the earth.

And I had the revelation (beheld and lo) that within the midst of my spiritual body (throne), my natural body (four beasts), and my spiritual mind (elders) was Jesus, the one who died for me (Lamb as it had been slain). I understood that he has perfect and complete (seven) power and knowledge (seven horns and seven eyes) and he is the perfect and complete (seven) Holy Spirit (seven Spirits of God) sent to me just as he promised his disciples that he would come (sent forth into all the earth).

Chapter six

Removing the Sin Nature

Rev 5:7 And he came and took the book out of the right hand of him that sat upon the throne.

We have already seen in the first verse of this chapter that the book represents our natural mind. The person in whom all this is taking place had been trying to rule his own life by his own understanding and natural ways and was therefore in the place of authority within himself. He finally came to the end of himself through the difficulties of life such that he was ready to give over the control of his life to Jesus. He realized that he did not understand himself and could not change himself. After he had exhausted his attempts to find help from some other source, he was finally ready to hand over the control of his life to Jesus. After he had cried out for help and wept over his own inadequacy, Jesus could see that this person was ready to give the place of authority in his life over to him. At this point Jesus takes the authority over this person's natural mind that has been handed to him. The right hand would represent the place of power and control and now this person no longer has that place of authority. Now Jesus is the one sitting on the throne as we will see in Rev 5:13.

I am now in the place of the writing of this book where I

need to tell of my own experience of this chapter. (As I explained earlier, I had intended for Revelation 4 and Revelation 5 to be two separate booklets but later combined them into one book. Even though I described my experience of the Lord's awakening related to Revelation 4, I decided to leave my description of it here also as it helps explain in context the difficult concepts I am relating in Revelation 5.)

If I had not experienced these things I would not have been able to understand the book of Revelation as I do now. Without the understanding I am about to give it might appear from my interpretation of this verse that Jesus has taken over this person's life completely such that the natural mind is no longer functional. This is not the case. There comes a time in our relationship with God, (and this is only for the church of the end times), when we have been through enough experiences with God that he knows we are totally yielded to him and that he has permission to direct us in all experiences of life. In the course of this new level of direction, we will be changed such that our sin nature will gradually be removed. Jesus will only do this with our permission and our cooperation. The difference is that communication with him has come to a new level where he can now instruct us in every little detail of life. It is a process whereby we are perfected and Jesus lives and moves in us in ever increasing measure.

This is not easy to explain because it involves a whole new level of spiritual experience that is presently not known by the church but will have to be known if we are to survive the cataclysmic events beginning to engulf all civilizations and societies and the whole natural earth. This mortal must put on immortality (1 Corinthians 15) and in order to do so we must be completely sin free. This has never before been possible because of the sin nature that indwells all persons and all of nature. God will first be lifting this curse off his people and then eventually, I believe, off the earth. (I have seen this in many of my deep Bible studies which would require long teachings and contextual presentations using allegory such as I am writing here in order to be understood.) As we cooperate with God, he will do this work in us. The deeper level of communication I am speaking of requires an awakening of parts of ourselves that "died" when Adam and Eve sinned.

The Lord told them that in the day they ate from the tree of the knowledge of good and evil they would surely die. A surface reading of Genesis would lead one to believe they didn't die that very day but only several hundred years later. The way I always explained this was that with the Lord one day is as a thousand years and a thousand years is as one day. Therefore, no one lived a thousand years after the original sin was committed. In this way they did die on the day they sinned. However, I now see a deeper interpretation of this and that is that the spiritual side of them actually did die at the time of their sin. They lost all perception of their spiritual body and spiritual mind which actually did die and that is why they lost their place in the garden. The garden of Eden is not a geographical location but a spiritual place that one can only enter once Jesus awakens their spiritual body and spiritual mind. These will only be awakened when the process of complete sanctification begins with our giving over the control of our own life to Jesus. As we hand him the book we are giving him authority over our life to a greater degree than has ever been possible. This will involve him awakening our spiritual body and spiritual mind. Every Christian has had his spiritual mind awakened partially, but the spiritual mind is far more vast than we can imagine and Jesus will awaken it in increments corresponding to our yieldedness to him. At the same time he will be gradually erasing our sin nature.

The awakening of the spiritual body is a distinct event that I believe every true believer in Christ will experience. This will signal the beginning of their entrance into a whole new realm in God. I had this experience in February of 1997. I believe the Lord allowed me to experience this before others so I could research it in the Word and prepare books and articles to help others understand their own experience when it happens.

In 1997, when I had this experience, I had been ministering for a year to a woman in our church who had been severely abused by the Illuminati and people in high political places all over the world. Before describing the experience, I would like to give some background information leading up to it. I had only been working with her for a few months when we attended and roomed together at a women's retreat our denomination was sponsoring in a nearby city. The first morning there we were in our room praying silently before the meetings commenced. She was sitting on the bed and I was sitting at a desk with my back to her. I had just finished silently asking the Lord for a double portion of his Spirit, when she said, "I just had a vision. I saw Jesus come to you and put two beautiful cloaks on you. One was red and the other was purple."

That was the beginning of an amazing experience with God that was beyond anything I could have imagined. This lady was incredibly broken which necessitated my working with her every day. The ministry was quite supernatural. The Lord himself would minister directly to her as I prayed. There were many powerful demons I had to cast out. Each time after I ministered to her, Jesus would give her a vision for me. He would say lovely things to me regarding what he thought of me and how much he loved me. In the visions he would bring me gifts...sometimes flowers, a ring, bracelets, or something appropriate to some life situation I was in. These were not actual, tangible things I received but just images depicting his love for me. Looking back later I could see what I did not understand at the time and that is that he was courting me like a bridegroom would court his prospective bride.

After this had been going on for a year, she had a vision of a wedding where Jesus and I were married. I felt nothing. It was just a lovely vision. I had no idea where this was all leading. A few days after the wedding vision, she had another vision where Jesus and I were sitting together on a big rock in a lovely meadow. We had been sitting there talking when he reached down, touched my feet and said, "There feet will never touch the ground again."

That night when I was relaxed in bed waiting for sleep to come, I thought about the vision of that day. What could it mean that my feet would never touch the ground again? Suddenly I felt a delightful tingling in my feet. It was very rhythmic and gentle. It spread up my legs, into the trunk of my body and into my arms and hands. My whole body felt as though it was being gently massaged deep inside. It was a feeling of deep love that could only come from Jesus. I felt his love all over my body. This feeling definitely had intelligence and was purposed. I knew I was experiencing something reserved for the church of the end times. I realized that Jesus had come to me and awakened my spiritual body.

I had known about the spiritual body because of my ministry to severely abused persons. The demons come to them in satanic rituals and awaken their spiritual bodies to unimaginable terror, pain and suffering. This awakening enables them to see and feel demons, but this is another deep subject I will only mention here to explain why I knew about the spiritual body and that mine was awakened. The wonderful feeling of that experience has never stopped. It has intensified and expanded to include many other manifestations of God's love.

With the awakening of the spiritual body, our ability to experience Jesus is greatly increased. Through my friend's visions the Lord trained me to know that he was communicating with me through various touches. For example, she had a vision of Jesus pouring anointing oil over my head. Then for the next two days or so I could feel every few minutes something gentle and warm coming down over my head to my shoulders. It was only happening to my spiritual body. It was very definite but deep inside and tingly not at all something felt by my natural body.

Concomitant to this experience, I was involved in daily, deep Bible studies for several hours every morning. I would take whole chapters of the Bible, look up every word in the original language and research it in every possible way known to me. I had always wanted to study the Bible in depth but didn't really know how to do it. Looking back to that time, I can see that these experiences with Jesus were definitely opening my spiritual mind related to the Scriptures. I was not searching the Scriptures looking for an understanding of what had happened to me. I was just doing my normal studies, but everywhere I studied I began to see, hidden in allegory and original language definitions, words associated with the gentle movement I experienced at the awakening of my spiritual body.

As I saw this I became more than ever convinced that Jesus intends this experience for all his people in the end times. I am very grateful that I was chosen to have it early so I could prepare these teachings. I was led through the veils into this experience by my friend's visions. Not everyone will have such an opportunity. Therefore, my writings will help others understand when they experience it.

This experience is not an end in itself but merely the beginning of a process we must all go through to become conformed to his image without spot or wrinkle. Further on in this chapter I will explain how Jesus communicates with me in almost a moment by moment discourse.

Verse and Interpretation

Rev 5:7 And he came and took the book out of the right hand of him that sat upon the throne.

At this point Jesus took authority over my natural mind because I chose to hand it over to him. He took it out of my right hand which represents the place of power and control and now I no longer had that place of authority. Now Jesus would be the one sitting on the throne.

* * * * * * * * * * * * * * * * * *

Rev 5:8 And when he had taken the book, the four beasts and four and twenty elders fell down before the Lamb, having every one of them harps, and golden vials full of odours, which are the prayers of saints.

According to the interpretation I have given thus far, the four beasts represent our natural body and the twenty-four elders our spiritual mind. When we give Jesus authority over our life by handing the book (representing our natural mind) to him, we will want to do as we see in this verse and that is to fall down before him. If you will remember, when I first felt the presence of the Lord awakening my spiritual body, I was lying in bed waiting to fall asleep. To be more precise, I was lying on my back at the time this happened. Although I feel the presence of the Lord at all times, the feeling is intensified whenever I return to the position I was in when this awakening first happened and that is lying down on my back. When we think of the four beasts and the twenty four elders falling down in the presence of Jesus, we think of them falling forward with their faces toward the ground. However, when I desire to spend special time with Jesus, I prefer to "fall down" by lying on my back. For me that could mean sitting back in a recliner-type chair with my feet extended or leaning back on our loveseat with my head on the armrest. For me this is falling down in his presence.

When I lean back in this way with the intent of spending time with Jesus, the feeling I have is incredibly wonderful and supernatural. I feel as though I am flying! I don't go anywhere physically and I am conscious of being in my living room the entire time. I'm not floating out of my body or looking down at myself from the ceiling, but I feel very much what I feel when a jet airliner takes off. However, what I am feeling with Jesus is much better than that. (It is interesting that the Greek word for 'fall down," *pipto*, comes from a root word, *petomai,* which means "to fly.") So this is how my natural body, allegorically represented here as the four beasts, falls down before Jesus, the Lamb. However, the twenty-four elders also fall down. Next we will see what that means.

The twenty-four elders represent our spiritual mind. How does our spiritual mind fall down before Jesus? The word "before" used here is *enopion* which means "in the presence of." There is no doubt once I intend to spend time with Jesus and my natural body falls down before him, that I am immediately in a deeper level of his presence than what I usually feel (which is also fantastic, but I have not yet touched on that here.) So for my spiritual mind to fall down before him, I make a conscious decision to focus my mind on Jesus. I do this by picturing him in my holy imagination and purposefully begin to imagine being with him in a beautiful place in heaven.

I no longer receive special prophetic words from my friend who led me through the veils as I mentioned earlier. She has been healed of her abuse and we no longer meet for ministry. It has been six years or more since I have received any of her prophetic messages on a regular basis. However, at the time when I was receiving them the Lord gave me repeated encouragement to practice visualizing him and thereby begin to develop my holy imagination. One of the most important features of our spiritual mind is our holy imagination. I have seen this fact reinforced over and over again in my deep allegorical Bible studies.

Since 1997 I have daily worked at developing my holy imagination. I have learned to see Jesus in my spiritual mind and I have developed many places of beauty and peace in my spiritual mind. Once our spiritual body has been awakened, a deeper level of our spiritual mind is also awakened. Both are immature at first and must go through a process of maturation as we focus on our relationship with Jesus and spend time in his presence. (I have seen this detailed in many of my studies and have written about it in my book *The Four Living Creatures*. I also saw much about it in my study on the tabernacle which I describe in my 18 hour video series offered free on my website.)

So once I fall down in his presence and feel myself flying, I immediately focus my mind on Jesus. In my spiritual mind I enter into a beautiful garden or his house or some other lovely place I have developed in my spiritual mind with the Lord's help. (We are to initiate the process of developing this place of beauty and God helps us develop it.) As soon as my mind focuses on Jesus, his presence becomes much stronger. I talk with him silently in my spiritual mind as I visualize being with him in one of these places. I have gone to these places thousands of times and they now seem very real to me. As I talk with him in my mind, he speaks to me in my awakened spiritual body. I do not hear his voice but he speaks by his presence which I feel in my body. For example, I might be praying about some situation, and at some point in the conversation I feel his presence come down on my right shoulder. I have learned that this means "yes" or that I am right about something. If I feel my nose start to tickle like it does before I sneeze, I know he is saying "no." This way of communicating has been invaluable to me.

Our Revelation verse states further, regarding the four beasts and the twenty-four elders, that they have harps and golden vials full of odours, which are the prayers of saints. Harps in Scripture are often identified with worship. For me the understanding goes a little deeper. In the Old Testament, the word harp is defined as coming from a root word meaning "to twang," and that, I think, is a good description of how it is played. The strings, after being plucked, vibrate and produce sound waves. However, in this case I am not speaking about sound waves but about "feeling waves." The waves I feel when I fall down in the presence of the Lord are not fast vibrations but very slow and more like the ebb and flow of waves on a large body of water. It will help our understanding to read the following definition of sound waves:

> A sound wave is the pattern of disturbance caused by the movement of energy traveling through a medium (such as air, water, or any other liquid or solid matter) as it propagates away from the source of the sound. The source is some object that causes a vibration, such as a ringing telephone, or a person's vocal chords. The vibration disturbs the particles in the surrounding medium; those particles disturb those next to them, and so on. The pattern of the disturbance creates outward movement in a wave pattern, like waves of seawater on the ocean. The wave carries the sound energy through the medium, usually in all directions and less intensely as it moves farther from the source. (Rouse)

Any time when I am still (such as now as I sit here writing) I feel a slow wavelike motion all through my body which is more pronounced when I "fall down before the Lord" as described above. As in the definition of a sound wave above, I feel "the movement of energy traveling through a medium" with the medium being my body. Jesus is the source of the wavelike motion. It is as though I am the harp and Jesus is plucking the strings. "The particles being disturbed in the surrounding medium" correspond to the sin nature that indwells my body. Regarding this sin nature in my body, "the pattern of disturbance creates outward movement in a wave pattern, like waves of seawater on the ocean. The wave carries the (elide 'sound') energy through the medium (my body) usually in all directions..." This is how the Lord gently removes the sin nature from our body. When I decided to find a good definition for sound waves and came across this one the first place I looked, I was absolutely amazed at how perfectly this scientific explanation of sound waves coincides with the spiritual reality going on in my body.

If there are any doubts that Jesus is the source of the wavelike motion, let's look back at the description of Jesus in Rev 4:2, 3: "And immediately I was in the spirit; and, behold, a throne was set in heaven, and one sat on the throne. And he that sat was to look upon like a jasper and a sardine stone..." If you will remember from Revelation 4, I did not see Jesus with my natural eyes, but my knowledge that he had come to me and was speaking to me came through feeling in my body. This is how I recognized (saw) him as a jasper stone according to the definition of jasper in the Hebrew which is "to polish". To polish is to rub something with a soft cloth with repetitive motion. I felt a rhythmic gentle motion like I was the one being polished. When we polish something we are rubbing away its tarnish, nicks and crannies or imperfections. Over time as I studied the Word, I came to understand that this gentle polishing motion that never stopped was Jesus' tender way of polishing away the weakness of sin nature inherent in my body. This has been going on for years now. I have strength, vitality and good health beyond anything I've ever known even as a young person. I still have a sin nature, but something supernatural is occurring in my body.

Not only was Jesus like a jasper when John saw him, but he was also like a sardine stone. The red color of this stone would be symbolic of Jesus' love for us—the love that led him to die for us on the cross. The feeling of God's love that came to me with the awakening of my spiritual body was profound and formerly unknown to me. I've felt loved all my life because I went from loving parents to a kind, loving husband, but I've never felt anything to compare with the love I feel from Jesus at all times. It is beyond description.

It is easy to see that what I wrote in Revelation 4 likening the feeling of the motion to the gentle polishing of a gem is another way of describing the wavelike motion of sound waves related to the plucking of the strings of a harp. In Revelation 4 we are the gem that Jesus is polishing; in Revelation 5 we are the harp Jesus is playing.

It is most astounding and exciting to think that Jesus is removing our sin nature from our bodies. We know about the process of sanctification whereby we are gradually perfected in our soul, but we tend not to think about anything of that nature going on correspondingly in our bodies, but it is time for this to take place. This is the redemption of the body reserved for the church of the end times (Rom 8:23). This is this mortal putting on immortality (1 Cor 15:53). This is the process we must go through in order to enter into God's kingdom that is coming on earth, and this is the only way we will survive the horrendous destruction of our planet, the pollution of our food and water, and all the other evils the Devil has been instructing the Antichrist's followers to promulgate on the peoples of the world. They are attempting via satanic rituals, DNA tampering, combining humans with machines, humans with demons, humans with animals and other vile scientific and spiritual "advances" to transcend themselves onto some higher plain of immortality and authority over the world. All Christians need to do is love and obey Jesus and he will lift us up into a heavenly dimension of love, peace and great power where we will do great exploits and even greater miracles than he did (John 14:12).

The last portion of Rev 5:8 states that they had "golden vials full of odours, which are the prayers of saints." As I have already explained, this verse is about the natural body (four beasts) and the spiritual mind (twenty-four elders). I described what the body feels as it falls down before Jesus and now the gold vials describe what the spiritual mind is experiencing when falling down in the presence of Jesus. A vial is a container. Our thoughts contain messages and understandings that we bring before Jesus as prayer. The fact that these thoughts are golden reveals that they are pure, and what could be more pure than picturing Jesus in our mind and expressing to him our love and appreciation for him. As we use our holy imagination to picture being with Jesus, the feeling of his presence intensifies. Over time as we do this on a daily basis, more of the spiritual mind is awakened. We are able to focus unswervingly on him and our visions of Jesus become clearer.

Verse and Interpretation

Rev 5:8 And when he had taken the book, the four beasts and four and twenty elders fell down before the Lamb, having every one of them harps, and golden vials full of odours, which are the prayers of saints.

When I gave Jesus authority over my natural mind (when Jesus had taken the book), Jesus was then on the throne of my life. This opened to me a new experience reserved for the church of the end times wherein when I would lie down, my natural body would feel the sensation of flying without actually leaving its physical environment, while my spiritual mind would focus on being in heaven with Jesus (the four beasts and the four and twenty elders fell down). There was the constant feeling of wavelike motion in my body. This was the Lord gently removing the sin nature from my body which would take place over a long period of time (harps). My thoughts were focused on Jesus as I expressed my love and appreciation for him in my holy imagination (prayers of the saints).

Chapter Seven

Heaven Is with Us

Rev 5:9 And they sung a new song, saying, Thou art worthy to take the book, and to open the seals thereof: for thou wast slain, and hast redeemed us to God by thy blood out of every kindred, and tongue, and people, and nation;

To sing a new song is to worship God in a new way which is now possible because of the great revelation of God and his love that has come to this person through the awakening of the spiritual side of his being. The Greek word for "new" used here is *kainos* which means "recently made, fresh, unprecedented, unheard of, that which as recently made is superior to what it succeeds." Before this experience we may have needed certain "props" to feel that we were getting into worship. Perhaps we needed to listen to Christian CDs in order to worship. Maybe we felt the need to be in a church packed with people and a professional worship team with the volume cranked up on the amplifiers in order to feel we were worshiping. All of that becomes unnecessary now that Jesus has come to us personally in an unprecedented way that is far beyond anything we could have ever imagined.

We no longer worship out of obedience whether we feel like it or not. Now we always feel like worshiping God. Anytime we are quiet before the Lord, his presence upon us intensifies and is felt by us in such a way that we are instantly focused on him and desiring to worship. We don't need Christian music or need to be with other people. Worship becomes immediate the minute our thoughts turn to Jesus. This feeling is such that we know he is with us and is receiving our worship.

Before this experience we may have felt inadequate to express our love for God because of a limited vocabulary. We may have felt we were just saying the same words over and over. Now there really is no need for words because all we need to do is focus our holy imagination on his face and the feelings of love for him are almost overwhelming. We can even feel that he receives our love.

Another amazing thing about this new worship is that what was once faith has become fact. I used to worship by faith believing that God heard and received my worship. Now I know for a fact that he does. We no longer need to believe by faith that God is always with us. We know for a fact he is always with us because the feeling of his presence never leaves. The gentle wavelike motion I spoke of earlier never stops. The feeling of his love is constant. In any difficult situation this sensation of his presence intensifies. In any situation in which I might feel threatened, I feel his warmth spread over my whole body. He is saying that he will protect me and I have nothing to worry about. I need to clarify that I don't mean to say we no longer need faith at all as there are always new challenges that require faith as we move upward in Christ.

I feel certain that what I am describing here is just the beginning. There is much, much more for us to experience of God's presence, power, protection and love. The more we decrease and he increases, the better it will get. Also the further we enter into the great tribulation of these end times, the more we are going to need God's presence and direction. He will give us what we need when we need it...and we will need faith to believe this because the events we will see going on around us as the New World Order tries to take over will be horrific. I have learned over the years that evil and good increase concurrently and in balance. When we hear about the evil, we need to know there is greater good that is just not being reported.

As the persons who have had this experience with Jesus worship him they are saying, "Thou art worthy to take the book, and to open the seals thereof: for thou wast slain, and hast redeemed us to God by thy blood out of every kindred, and tongue, and people, and nation;"

The experience they are having with Jesus in this new spiritual dimension is such that there is absolutely no doubt in their mind as to the ability or trustworthiness of Jesus to take care of any and all things that pertain to their life. They know he died on the cross that they might draw near to him, and now they are experiencing a nearness they never dreamed possible. To open the seals will be to take these people into perfection. They are most appreciative of the price Jesus paid to be able to do this for them. Once they went through their struggle as explained in the first few verses of this chapter of Revelation, they learned they will always be totally dependent on Jesus for all things. They know Jesus is there for them and he has what they need that no one else can give them. This kind of dependence is a sure sign they are on the path to maturity and wholeness in Christ.

This experience with Jesus is deeply personal and intimate but can be happening to many people at the same time all over the world. Jesus loves all people with no regard for their family of origin, the language they speak, their education, race or nationality.

Verse and Interpretation

Rev 5:9 And they sung a new song, saying, Thou art worthy to take the book, and to open the seals thereof: for thou wast slain, and hast redeemed us to God by thy blood out of every kindred, and tongue, and people, and nation;

The people who have had this end-time experience of the awakening of the spiritual side of their being enabling them to experience God's presence and love continually will be able to worship God in a way never before possible (sung a new song). Jesus, because of who he is and what he has done for us (worthy), is able to reveal to us what is in our heart (take the book and open the seals). He is doing this for people all over the world (every kindred, tongue, people, and nation).

* *

Rev 5:10 And hast made us unto our God kings and priests: and we shall reign on the earth.

When Jesus reveals to us what is in our heart, we know to repent and clear our heart of anything that is not like Jesus. As we do so, he gradually becomes our life. His thoughts become our thoughts and we become like him. This is why we can be kings and priests and why we can reign on earth. The decisions we make will not be our own decisions but Jesus'. Our ministry will not flow forth from our own will and volition, but from Jesus'. This will be a work of God in us that we cannot do ourselves. However, we will have our part in that we are to obey God, submit to him and prepare ourselves in whatever ways God directs.

I believe those of us alive at this time are going to experience the end of the world as we know it and the coming of the Kingdom of God on earth. It is comforting to know that God will have people ruling that are so filled with his Spirit that their decisions will be his decisions. In Luke, Jesus tells of a nobleman who went to a far country to receive for himself a kingdom and return. Upon leaving he gave ten pounds to ten servants and expected them to be productive and give him increase upon his return. To those who did as instructed he said, "Well done, thou good servant: because thou hast been faithful in a very little, have thou authority over ten cities," and to another he said, "Be thou also over five cities." However to the one who chose to do nothing with what he had been given, the king expressed his anger and took away what this unproductive one had and gave it to the one who had earned the most. There are many things one can learn from Jesus' teaching here, but the point I want to make is that God is going to have faithful and proven persons in his kingdom who will rule the world in righteousness. I truly believe we will see that happen after everything falls. God cannot build his kingdom on top of the Devil's kingdom. First he must tear down that which the Devil has built up and then establish his own righteous kingdom in its place.

Currently we are seeing the destruction of our present world due to the insane decisions being made by world leaders. The most current nonsensical decision is the bringing down of borders such that Muslims are flooding into nations bringing their violence and Sharia law with them. Western civilization is crumbling as a result of these incomprehensible decisions. I have no doubt there will be worldwide Jihad against all Christians and non-Muslims. And yet, knowing the greatness of God, one can only trust that this will all work according to his plan to judge the world and prepare his bride for his coming. The Lord prophesied to our church in 1972 that he was going to shake the world and that nothing would be left standing except that which was rooted and grounded in him. Surely the nations of the world are not standing on the Rock, the Lord Jesus Christ, so they have to come down. The Muslims are one powerful factor, among others, currently bringing them down. If we have myopic vision such that we only see the destruction engulfing the world, we have reason to fear. If we have higher vision to see the metanarrative of God at work to accomplish his plan in the earth, then we should have nothing to fear.

Verse and Interpretation

Rev 5:10 And hast made us unto our God kings and priests: and we shall reign on the earth.

God's faithful people will be so filled with his Spirit that they will reign on earth and minister according to his perfect will with no selfish motives or error.

* * * * * * * * * * * * * * *

Rev 5:11 And I beheld, and I heard the voice of many angels round about the throne and the beasts and the elders: and the number of them was ten thousand times ten thousand, and thousands of thousands;

Now that this person living in the end times has come to this state of perfection, God is able to open his eyes to see into the heavenly realm that has been kept closed until perfection comes. Perfection comes only when we have died to self completely. The sin nature that came into humankind at the time of the Fall can only be defeated through death. It can never be improved or converted. It must die. When Jesus destroyed the Devil by his death (Heb 2:14), he made it possible for us to follow him to this place of sinless perfection through our own death—our death to self. In ages past this was only possible to a certain degree. For Christians living in the end times who are willing to sacrifice all for Jesus, this will become a reality. It is a work that only God can do but it requires our cooperation.

We must be dead to self to see into this heavenly dimension. This is because we see spiritual things through the eyes of our heart rather than our natural eyes. If there is any darkness at all in our heart, it is possible for us to be deceived because, as the Bible tells us, Satan can transform himself into an angel of light (2 Cor 11:14). As Jesus taught, it is the pure in heart who will see God (Matt 5:8). John tells us that when Christ shall appear we shall be like him for we shall see him as he is and this requires purifying our hearts (1 John 3:2, 3).

As we progress further into these end times realizing the proliferation of the New World Order, we are going to need the assistance of angels. When our every move is watched by cameras, satellites, and drones and when those who refuse the mark of the beast are targeted for extermination, we will need heaven's assistance to know when to come and go, whom to trust, where to be safe and all manner of other important guidance and provision. I truly believe those who have passed into heaven before us are aware of us and our situations and will be assisting us in many ways. When one considers that the UN's Agenda 21 (or as it seems to have been renamed Agenda 2030) mandates that the human population be culled from almost seven billion people to just 500 million, the implications are mind boggling. And yet all things are known by God and if we are trusting in him, we need have no fear.

We may be sure that Christians will be targeted for extermination in America as they already are in some other nations. We may feel powerless and alone in the face of the armies of Russia and China that are already in this country (and have been seen and photographed by many persons) and the militant Muslims being brought into this country by Obama, but they who are with us are more than they that are against us. Elisha knew this. When the Syrian army came against him, God opened the eyes of his servant to see the armies of heaven with them:

> And Elisha prayed, and said, Lord, I pray thee, open his eyes, that he may see. And the Lord opened the eyes of the young man; and he saw: and, behold, the mountain was full of horses and chariots of fire round about Elisha. And when they came down to him, Elisha prayed unto the Lord, and said, Smite this people, I pray thee, with blindness. And he smote them with blindness according to the word of Elisha (2 Kings 6:17, 18).

I have often thought about the possibility that should our

enemies come against us, we might be able to pray and have God blind their eyes so they could not approach us. I was thinking about this again in church Sunday while people were giving testimonies of answered prayer. All of a sudden, I couldn't see! It was not that everything went dark, but it was like there was a division between my right eye and left eye such that nothing fit together and one side was higher than the other. Had I been standing, I might have fallen down it was so powerful. It only lasted a few seconds and my vision came back to normal. I believe God was saying to me that he can certainly blind the eyes of whomsoever he chooses just as he did in Elisha's time.

My husband and I get our news from alternative news sites online and totally ignore the mainstream media news because we choose not to hear their lies or propaganda. God also supernaturally shows us things. As I wrote previously in Revelation 4, I saw in a dream/vision in 2010 the foreign troops in our nation coming after the American people with their weapons in hand. I was shown this twice. Two is the number of witness in the Bible, so I knew this was certain. Since that time I have read accounts of those who have actually seen them and even photographed them.

There is a concerted effort by the Obama administration to wipe out our 2nd Amendment right to bear arms. Anyone who knows history knows that whenever a populace is disarmed by their government, genocide follows. One can see online pictures of hundreds of thousands of black plastic coffins stacked outside many of our largest cities. Obviously our government anticipates these will be needed when millions of Americans die.

No matter what happens, we need to focus on Jesus

Christ and his Word. As we obediently look to him, our faith will grow and our hearts will be purified. Then God will be able to part the veil for us to see the hosts of heaven that are all around us, and, as I explained earlier in this book, his presence is going to be with us in a powerful and comforting way never before known to the church. We, the church of the end times, will be entering a realm of God reserved for this time—the time of the return of Christ and the purification of his bride.

The Beasts and the Elders

It is important to notice that the beasts and the elders are in the presence of all these angels. The beasts, if you will remember, represent our physical body. The elders represent our spiritual mind. The fact that they are in this heavenly realm with the angels suggests to me that our physical bodies and spiritual minds are going to be in a dimension of God not before possible. Is this a realm Philip briefly entered when he left the Ethiopian eunuch and was immediately at another place? Is this where the disciples were with Jesus when he got in their boat and they were immediately at the other side of the sea? I believe this is a distinct possibility.

We are used to traveling at will around our nation and in other countries. We get in our automobile, make sure it is full of gas and take off for wherever we want to be. Our daughters live in other states several hours drive in opposite directions from where we presently reside. We try to visit each twice a year for a total of four trips. We minister in a city over an hour's drive from where we live. Will we be able to do this in the future? Not if the purveyors of the NWO have their way.

Already there are experiments going on in the US where people are paying a tax for every mile they drive. A device is installed in their automobile that keeps a record of miles driven. As the draconian measures of Agenda 21 are imposed on us, we can be certain that our use of fossil fuels will be greatly curtailed. There is no way wind and solar power can replace fossil fuels. I am certain that when God wants us to minister, he will see to it that we go where he is directing no matter what constraints are placed on us.

Verse and Interpretation

Rev 5:11 And I beheld, and I heard the voice of many angels round about the throne and the beasts and the elders: and the number of them was ten thousand times ten thousand, and thousands of thousands;

Once Christ has become our very life, God is able to lift the veil and permit us to see and hear things in the heavenly realm that is nearby but has been hidden from our senses. We will see that there are more that are with us than those that are against us. We are surrounded by angels too numerous to count. Our physical body (four beasts) and our spiritual mind (24 elders) will also be in this heavenly dimension.

* *

Rev 5:12 Saying with a loud voice, Worthy is the Lamb that was slain to receive power, and riches, and wisdom, and strength, and honour, and glory, and blessing.

To witness such worship would be a thrill unequalled by anything a person could experience on earth. I can't help but think that in the context of this Rev 5 passage, this worship may be related to what has been happening throughout this chapter, specifically that a person representative of the church of the end times has relinquished control of his own life and been raised up by God into this heavenly dimension. I believe the great church that has passed over before us is mindful of us and desirous of participating with us in the great end time battles. They would rejoice to see us enter into this heavenly realm and would know that only Jesus could make this possible. They might be glorifying God for the great work he has done in his church. I should think worship would go on continually in heaven, but this particular occasion might be related to this great victory God has brought forth in his people in the end times that we might be there also to join in this magnificent worship.

The Bible tells us that angels are ministering spirits sent forth to aid the people of God on earth. Therefore they would probably be aware of all that is taking place with the church now including the fact that much of the church has succumbed to deception and idolatry. However, for those Christians who have remained true to the faith, we can expect to experience that which we see here in this verse. Not only will we experience heavenly worship with angels and departed saints, but also, as I stated earlier, they will be assisting us as we face the challenges of the NWO.

I am reminded of a scripture in Genesis where angels came to Jacob just after he parted from Laban and was facing his brother Esau. There was trepidation in his heart because the last time he had seen Esau, Esau was threatening to kill him.

And Jacob went on his way, and the angels of God met him. And when Jacob saw them, he said, This is God's host: and he called the name of that place Mahanaim (Gen 32:1, 2).

Mahanaim means "two hosts" or "two armies." Jacob must have been greatly encouraged to know he was not alone. The army of heaven was with him, and they will also be with us. One of our greatest weapons against the enemy is worship. When we worship, we are not alone as the angels and departed saints in heaven are also worshiping at the same time. We know this by faith, but I believe we will actually experience it as we enter more deeply into the events of the end times.

Verse and Interpretation

Rev 5:12 Saying with a loud voice, Worthy is the Lamb that was slain to receive power, and riches, and wisdom, and strength, and honour, and glory, and blessing.

As the veil is lifted and we see the angels in heaven, this verse shows us what they are doing. They are worshiping God. Although I believe this is probably going on continuously in heaven, they may be worshiping specifically in this passage related to the context of Rev 5 where a believer from the end times has been able to join with them in this worship because of the completed work of Christ in his life.

* * * * * * * * * * * * * * * * * * * *

Rev 5:13 And every creature which is in heaven, and on the earth, and under the earth, and such as are in the sea, and all that are in them, heard I saying, Blessing, and honour, and glory, and power, be unto him that sitteth upon the throne, and unto the Lamb for ever and ever.

As related to the context of this chapter and my interpretation, I believe all things that have life, all creatures in heaven, those on the earth, under the earth and in the sea can now be understood as having a significant purpose in the plan of God for this person's life and for all humanity. Now that this person is able to be in heaven with the veil lifted, he sees all of life as he has never seen it before. No longer does he separate creation or his own life into good and bad, but he sees all things from God's perspective. All things have had their place in the preparation of this person, as representative of the church of the end times, in order for him to come into completion in Christ. Therefore, all these things have been turned into praise because without adversity (as well as the good things), he could not be here.

In our narrow view of life, we humans tend to eschew that which we deem "bad" and embrace all that we consider to be good. However, in God all these things have their purpose. Without the difficulties of life including pain, sorrow and suffering, we could never arrive at this place of standing in heaven in the presence of God joining in worship with the angels. This verse doesn't actually say he is joining in worship, but in these surroundings, he could not help but do so. One could not be in this environment without every fiber of his being joining in with this adoration of the one who saved him and brought him to this place of victory and glory. Every adversity has been an opportunity to rise up in Christ.

There is an enigmatic verse in Isaiah that can be understood in this context. "I form the light, and create darkness: I make peace, and create evil: I the LORD do all these things" (Isa 45:7). Does God really create evil? I've checked this verse in many different translations and they all agree that this is really what the verse says. This could only be explained to my understanding if we go all the way back to the question of the origin of the Devil. How did he get in the Garden of Eden in the first place? Is he really a fallen angel that rebelled against God and took a third of the angels with him? Or was he created by God to be just what he is in order to test people and give them the opportunity to choose evil or good? I tend to believe the latter. If we don't know what evil and adversity are, how can we choose for or against God? The teaching the church and even the unchurched seem to have embraced concerning the Devil being a rebellious fallen angel comes from Isaiah 14 regarding Lucifer. This is the only place in the Bible the word "Lucifer" appears. It has been widely taught that Lucifer is the Devil. If this is true, why is he never again referred to in Scripture by that name? However, there is another, and to my mind better, understanding taught by very few--that Lucifer is actually referring to Adam. There is an excellent teaching on this at the following website address: https://www.godfire.net/Lucifer.html

It is important to understand, I believe, that God does not go around creating evil. He created the Devil who is evil. (He was a murderer from the beginning [John 8:44]). He created humankind with free will and because of the Fall we all inherited a sin nature. All these things combined create evil.

Getting back to this verse in Revelation, this person now sees all things in life as related to the metanarrative of God. In other words, he sees the big picture. No longer is he focused on his immediate situation in his earthly life. From this new perspective with the veil lifted whereby he can enter into heaven, he now understands his entire life has been purposed by God. Each thing that came into his life was necessary for him to come into maturity. There had to be evil in order for him to reject it. There had to be adversity to show him his own inadequacy and need for Christ. He had to face temptations that revealed the darkness in his own heart so that he could see how far removed from God's standard for righteousness he actually was. He had to deny himself, take up his cross daily and follow Christ. Only through death to self and the formation of Christ's life within could he be in this place behind the veil experiencing heaven.

Verse and Interpretation

Rev 5:13 And every creature which is in heaven, and on the earth, and under the earth, and such as are in the sea, and all that are in them, heard I saying, Blessing, and honour, and glory, and power, be unto him that sitteth upon the throne, and unto the Lamb forever and ever.

As related to the context of this chapter, all things that have life can now be understood as having a significant purpose in the plan of God for this person's life and for all humanity. Now that this person is able to be in heaven with the veil lifted, he sees all of life as he has never seen it before. No longer does he separate creation or his own life into good and bad, but he sees all things from God's perspective. All things have had their place in the preparation of this person, as representative of the church of the end times, in order for him to come into completion in Christ. Therefore, all these things have been turned into praise because without adversity (as well as the good things), he could not be here.

* * * * * * * * * * * * * * *

Rev 5:14 And the four beasts said, Amen. And the four and twenty elders fell down and worshipped him that liveth for ever and ever.

I will restate this verse using our interpretation thus far for the four beasts and the twenty-four elders.

> And the physical body said, Amen. And the spiritual mind fell down and worshipped him that liveth for ever and ever.

I find this verse to be very exciting! For the physical body to say "Amen" means it is in total agreement with God and all he has done. My physical body is not yet agreeing with God. When the Word says, "By his stripes you were healed," parts of my body are not saying "Amen." There must come a time when our body will align itself with the Word of God because there is going to be the redemption of the body. We know this because the Word says so: "...we ourselves groan within ourselves, waiting for the adoption, to wit, the redemption of our body" (Rom 8:23b). Here is another scripture regarding this:

> Behold, I show you a mystery; we shall not all sleep, but we shall all be changed, In a moment, in the twinkling of an eye, at the last trump: for the trumpet shall sound, and the dead shall be raised incorruptible, and we shall be changed. For this corruptible must put on incorruption, and this mortal must put on immortality. So when this corruptible shall have put on incorruption, and this mortal shall have put on immortality,

then shall be brought to pass the saying that is written, Death is swallowed up in victory (1 Cor 15:51-54).

We can anticipate this to be something that occurs with the second coming of Christ.

> For our citizenship is in heaven, from which we also eagerly wait for the Savior, the Lord Jesus Christ, who will transform our lowly body that it may be conformed to His glorious body, according to the working by which He is able even to subdue all things to Himself (Phil 3:;20, 21 NKJV).

We know that even though the physical body dies, as has been the case with all those who have gone before us, people live on in their spiritual body in heaven or hell as the case may be. However, I believe we who are alive at the return of Christ will be perfected even in our physical body while on earth. Paul wrote the following to the Thessalonians: "And the very God of peace sanctify you wholly; and I pray God your whole spirit and soul and body be preserved blameless unto the coming of our Lord Jesus Christ" (1 Th 5:23).

Here are two Old Testament verses that indicate the redemption of the body:

> He will swallow up death in victory; and the Lord GOD will wipe away tears from off all faces; and the rebuke of his people shall he take away from off all the earth: for the LORD hath spoken it (Isa 25:8).

> I will ransom them from the power of the grave; I will redeem them from death: O death, I will be thy plagues; O grave, I will be thy destruction: repentance shall be hid from mine eyes (Hos 13:14).

I believe in our Revelation scripture here that when the four beasts say "Amen," the natural body is in agreement with all God has said and done. God has done a work in the body that has removed the curse of decay and death that came upon humankind at the fall. This victory in the body could only be accomplished in conjunction with the 24 elders bowing to Christ. The elders, interpreted here as being the spiritual mind, represent a fully matured spiritual mind since they are elders. When we come into full spiritual maturity in Christ (24 elders), there will be healing for our bodies (four beasts say amen). Until then, sickness is something that humbles us and causes us to seek God more fervently.

With the removal of the sin nature from the body, after the perfecting of the spirit, sickness and death will no longer be our lot in life. God will restore youthfulness to our bodies. This may sound preposterous to some people, but we need to see this in context of what is happening in our world right now. Our world is dying. Pollution, radiation poisoning, genetic alteration of our food, depletion of the ozone layer, and many other factors are killing off plant and animal life and such that much of our planet will soon be uninhabitable. And yet, our God is aware of all these things and all things work together to accomplish his purpose in the earth. He is allowing this as judgment on the wicked. Daniel tells us, "…there shall be a time of trouble, such as never was since there was a nation even to that same time: and at that time thy people shall be delivered, every one that shall be found written in the book." Surely this time of trouble is upon us. What form will this deliverance take? I believe it will be the removal of the curse we inherited from Adam and Eve. As the curse is lifted, we will grow younger. Consider the following scriptures:

> If there be a messenger with him, an interpreter, one among a thousand, to show unto man his uprightness: Then he is gracious unto him, and saith, Deliver him from going down to the pit: I have found a ransom. His flesh shall be fresher than a child's: he shall return to the days of his youth (Job 33:23-25).

Jesus Christ paid our ransom. When our redemption is completed on earth, we will find ourselves becoming younger instead of older.

> Bless the LORD, O my soul, and forget not all his benefits: Who forgiveth all thine iniquities; who healeth all thy diseases; Who redeemeth thy life from destruction; who crowneth thee with lovingkindness and tender mercies; Who satisfieth thy mouth with good things; so that thy youth is renewed like the eagle's (Psa 103:3-5).

What would the renewing of our youth have to do with an eagle? Eagles don't grow younger; therefore, I don't believe this has anything to do with their age. The main point I see here is that eagles tear flesh off their prey and eat it. Our flesh, our sin nature, must be torn away from us. When this sin nature is gone, we will no longer suffer sickness and aging. Perhaps this idea of the eagle eating, actually swallowing, flesh is tied in with the scriptures that say death will be swallowed up.

> He will swallow up death in victory; and the Lord GOD will wipe away tears from off all faces; and the rebuke of his people shall he take away from off all the earth: for the LORD hath spoken it (Isa 25:8).

So when this corruptible shall have put on incorruption, and this mortal shall have put on immortality, then shall be brought to pass the saying that is written, Death is swallowed up in victory (1 Cor 15:54).

2 Cor 5:4 For we that are in this tabernacle do groan, being burdened: not for that we would be unclothed, but clothed upon, that mortality might be swallowed up of life.

Our sin nature has everything to do with sickness, aging and death. Without a sin nature, none of these would be part of our lives. Jesus will take us through a process in these end times whereby the sin nature will be completely removed. It will require our cooperation with him as he reveals our sin to us and gradually burns it up as we go through a process of judgment.

Verse and Interpretation

Rev 5:14 And the four beasts said, Amen. And the four and twenty elders fell down and worshipped him that liveth forever and ever.

At last my physical body (four beasts) came into the perfection God intended for it as it aligned itself fully with all the scriptures related to the redemption of the body (said Amen). My spiritual mind (twenty four elders) was totally submitted to the will of God in complete humility such that it only wanted to fall down and worship God giving him full honor for all that he had done (worshiped him). I knew that because he lives forever and ever that I too would live forever because his life had become my life.

* * * * * * * * * * * * * * * * * * * *

In Revelation 4 and 5 we have seen that God will be awakening us and revealing things to us that the church of past ages was not permitted to know. In ensuing chapters of Revelation, when viewed allegorically and inwardly, details may be seen about the process we must go through to be perfected and conformed to the image of Christ. Outwardly they reveal great judgments in the earth. Inwardly they reveal things in our heart and body that must be removed or changed before we can be fully conformed to his image.

Chapter Eight

The White Horse and His Rider

Rev 6:1 And I saw when the Lamb opened one of the seals, and I heard, as it were the noise of thunder, one of the four beasts saying, Come and see.

As was explained previously the four beasts represent us, human beings, in our natural body living on earth in the end times. We are seen here in heaven because God is going to raise us up into a heavenly dimension in the end times even while we are still on earth. Our bodies are going to be changed. We are going to put off mortality and put on immortality. As I explained in Revelation 4 and 5, something happens in a moment, in the twinkling of an eye and we know that we have entered into a whole new dimension in God reserved for the church of the end times. This is only the beginning of a process we then go through, a process with God that requires our cooperation, which will result in our becoming the pure spotless bride for which he is returning.

The Noise of Thunder

John does not actually hear the noise of thunder. He hears something that he cannot accurately describe because it is "as it were the noise of thunder." To comprehend spiritually what he is trying to convey to us regarding what he heard we need to understand something about the nature of thunder. Thunder is caused by lightning. The electricity passes through the air and causes the molecules of air to vibrate resulting in sound. So by looking at a very basic understanding of thunder we find that it is a sound caused by vibration that is initiated by lightning. The dictionary of English words defines vibration as "a continuous, slight shaking movement."

Now let's take these natural terms and put them in a spiritual dimension. Jesus at his second coming is likened to lightning. "For as the lightning, that lighteneth out of the one part under heaven, shineth unto the other part under heaven; so shall also the Son of man be in his day" (Luke 17:24). So we could say that Jesus is the lightning. Lightning causes the vibration of air molecules that result in the sound of thunder. Jesus, the one who is all light in whom there is no darkness (lightning), will come to us in the end times and touch us resulting in a slight, continuous shaking movement (vibration [thunder]) in our body (beast).

This is the revelation of the first beast. The one on the white horse is Jesus. The revelation comes to us through the beast. The beast is our body. Jesus (lightning) comes to us personally and touches us and we feel our body come to life in a very slow, continuous shaking movement or vibration (thunder).

As I sit here in my chair writing this on December 27, 2015 in Indianapolis, Indiana, I hear thunder. It really is thundering…repeatedly. It ought to be cold here and precipitation should to be in the form of snow or ice of some sort. Instead it is raining and thundering. The sky is lighting up with lightning.

The White Horse and His Rider

As I write about lightning while listening to thunder, I think of 1 John 1:5, "This then is the message which we have heard of him, and declare unto you, that God is light, and in him is no darkness at all." I saw no light when he came to me that night of February 11, 1997 as I was lying in bed waiting for sleep to come. I only felt the results of that light.

As I lay there all relaxed, I began to feel a slow, gentle vibration type of movement begin in my feet and quickly spread throughout my entire body. I knew Jesus had touched me. He had awakened my body to feel his touch. This gentle movement has never left. The spiritual side of my body has been awakened by Jesus. I heard no sound and saw no light, but the message was powerful and there was no mistaking what God was saying to me. He was with me, he loved me deeply and he would never leave me.

This is the first seal opened and this is the first beast.

Verse and Interpretation

Rev 6:1 And I saw when the Lamb opened one of the seals, and I heard, as it were the noise of thunder, one of the four beasts saying, Come and see.

I realized that Jesus (Lamb) had come to me and opened something within me that had been sealed off from me (one of the seals). This new thing opened to me was the slow, continuous and gentle movement of my spiritual body (noise of thunder) that was within my natural body (four beasts). This new experience was communicating something to me (come and see).

* * * * * * * * * * * * *

Rev 6:2 And I saw, and behold a white horse: and he that sat on him had a bow; and a crown was given unto him:

and he went forth conquering, and to conquer.

The White Horse

Everything here is symbolic. Therefore, this is not really a horse; the horse is a symbol of something else. It would be difficult to identify exactly what this horse represents without identifying who is riding on the horse. We can identify the rider of the horse from Revelation 19:11: "And I saw heaven opened, and behold a white horse; and he that sat upon him was called Faithful and True, and in righteousness he doth judge and make war." This is none other than the Lord Jesus Christ. He is the one on the white horse in Revelation 19 and he is the one on the white horse in Revelation 6.

As we continue with our inward view, we will see that the white horse is part of us. Jesus has come to us in a new way by awakening our spiritual body. The white horse is our spiritual body. According to Scripture there are four bodies that all human beings have incorporated in their physical body: a natural body and a spiritual body (1 Cor 15:44); a body of sin (Rom 6:6) and a body of death (Rom 7:24). This understanding should help us unlock the mystery of the four horses and their riders.

Since it is the four beasts (the body) that are/is communicating with us when the seals are opened, and since the first horse represents one of the four bodies named in Scripture, then it should reasonably follow that the remaining three horses should also have something to do with our body:

- White horse = spiritual body
- Red horse = natural body
- Black horse = body of sin
- Pale horse = body of death

If you have a problem identifying your body with a horse, we can turn to Scripture for some support for this representation. However, most of these are hidden in allegory also. We will find (as we progress further into these end times and the mysteries of Scripture begin opening even more) that a thorough knowledge of the Bible is needed in order to understand these deeper revelations scripturally. Here are two scriptures that compare people to horses:

> I have compared thee, O my love, to a company of horses in Pharaoh's chariots (Song 1:9).

> They were as fed horses in the morning: every one neighed after his neighbour's wife (Jer 5:8).

This next one is hidden in allegory but I'll try to explain as briefly as I can:

> Dan shall judge his people, as one of the tribes of Israel. Dan shall be a serpent by the way, an adder in the path, that biteth the horse heels, so that his rider shall fall backward (Gen 49:16, 17).

Dan is one of Jacob's twelve sons. In my DVD on Jacob's Twelve Sons (that can be seen or purchased on my website) I reveal that each son, when thoroughly examined scripturally, represents a particular aspect of our inner being that God will bring to perfection in the end times. In this study, Dan represents our conscience. As we apply this knowledge to the passage from Genesis quoted above, we can see that Dan judges. Judging is a function of our conscience. In this type, we are the horse. Our conscience "bites at our heels" when we begin to do something we should not. We feel an irritation along with a sense that something is not right. This is the attempt of the conscience to get us to "fall back" from entering into the particular sin we are contemplating. Dan is not mentioned in the Book of Revelation with one reason being that when we come into perfection we will no longer need a conscience.

Jesus at his second coming is riding on a white horse which I have identified as being our spiritual body. Jesus is coming first of all in us. Our first indication that he has come to us is when our spiritual body is awakened as I recounted in Revelation 4 and again in Revelation 5. As I described in those chapters, I can literally feel Jesus gently descending on me from time to time. The movement I feel continually in my body could quite easily be likened to the gentle cantor of a spiritual horse in slow motion.

The concept of the oneness of Christ with his people is seldom emphasized in the church. The perception of disappearing off the earth in a Rapture or of seeing Jesus descending from the clouds is the usual emphasis regarding his second coming. The intimacy of marriage and the oneness of Christ with his people is little understood nor emphasized in our churches today.

This concept of Jesus coming to earth in his people, his body, is probably unknown to most Christians because it is seldom taught in the churches. The false doctrine of disappearing bodily off the earth in the Rapture has been the most common teaching for the end time church. Sadly this will leave many Christians totally devastated and spiritually lost when it doesn't happen. The experience of Jesus coming to us personally and awakening our spiritual body and then gently and repeatedly descending upon us over a period of many years is a rapturous experience to say the least, but we are not going to leave the earth behind. We are going to overcome all adversities and enter into the fullness of Christ here on earth.

Some scriptures that indicate Christ returning in his body, the church, are listed below:

Rom 8:18 For I reckon that the sufferings of this present time are not worthy to be compared with the glory which shall be revealed in us. (Some translators changed the word "in" to "to" but "in" is the more accurate translation.)

Col 3:4 When Christ, who is our life, shall appear, then shall ye also appear with him in glory.

1 John 3:2 Beloved, now are we the sons of God, and it doth not yet appear what we shall be: but we know that, when he shall appear, we shall be like him; for we shall see him as he is.

1 Cor 6:2 Do ye not know that the saints shall judge the world? and if the world shall be judged by you, are ye unworthy to judge the smallest matters?

The Bow

As this scripture indicates, he has a bow. When Jesus descends upon us ever so gently as he awakens our spiritual body, he has a bow. So what is the bow? One commentator I read suggested it was a rainbow. However, this is not accurate when we look at the Greek. There is a Greek word for rainbow but it is not used here. The Greek word for bow used here is *toxon* and it appears nowhere else in Scripture. The only information we are given by Strong is from the base of its derivative word meaning "apparently as the simplest fabric." If we were looking at this verse literally we might consider the bow to be a weapon that shoots arrows. However no arrows are mentioned. So what is the bow spiritually and how would Jesus use it in the context of this particular interpretation?

I turn now to examine this root word in its fullness not just its base because I believe God has a message for us in its root word *tikto*. It means "to produce (from seed, as a mother...etc.), lit. or fig.:--bear, be born, bring forth, be delivered, be in travail." Based on the meanings of this root word, I offer the following interpretation: He will break us down into the simplest fabric (*toxon*) with which he will produce something (*tikto*). He is going to produce a human being in absolute perfection who will be birthed (tikto) into his kingdom. I base this not only on the root word but also on the way I feel in my body. I have often thought that this blissful, gentle wave-like movement I feel continually in my body must be what a baby feels floating in its mother's womb.

The Crown

In order to birth us into his kingdom here on earth, he has to break us down into the simplest fabric (bow). Here is where the crown comes in. The crown "was given to him."

Who gave him the crown? The crown is a symbol of authority and we are the ones who give him the authority to do this in us. He knows by the way we live before him whether or not we are ready to give him authority to break us down into the simplest fabric from which he can make a perfect human being. Jesus never forces us to accept the cross. He never forces us to pledge our love to him. He gives us free will and never forces himself on us. When he comes to us as depicted allegorically here on the white horse, it is because we have demonstrated in our lives that we are going to go all the way into his fullness. Now he is going to help us achieve this. He does this by conquering all that is in us that holds us back from completeness in him. This requires our cooperation with him. He does the deep work in our heart but we have outward obediences we must perform that enable him to do this.

By way of illustration I will now relate to you a spiritual dream I was given many years ago shortly after his presence came to me in the awakening of my spiritual body. In this dream I saw a bird, a red cardinal to be exact, tightly encased in a clear plastic cylinder from which it could not escape. I saw a clear liquid come into the cylinder but there was not enough to drown him. As I watched, the bird's feathers began to drop off. Eventually all his pretty red feathers were gone. He turned into a worm and crawled down into the ground. I had the sense that the bird represented me.

I had no idea at the time what the dream meant, but over the years it became clear. I was doing a lot of things women in our culture do when attempting to look their best. One by one the Lord began to point out to me things I was doing that he would no longer permit me to do. I found this to be incredibly difficult and humiliating. Some of these things took years for me to overcome. His instructions that I was no longer permitted to wear any makeup was one of the hardest. It probably took around three years for me to finally feel comfortable with no makeup. There were other things I was instructed to give up that were not so difficult such as hair dye, perfume, jewelry and a lot of clothes. The last really big trial in this regard was when I was told I could no longer style my hair or look in a mirror. I was permitted to get my hair cut and comb it, but I could not style it with a brush, hair dryer or curling iron. I had to let it air dry after shampooing and no hairspray or styling gel was permitted…and absolutely no looking in the mirror. That has taken years to overcome—perhaps four or five.

There have been unpleasant consequences administered when I was disobedient. I learned to appreciate the words of the Psalmist, "Before I was afflicted I went astray: but now have I kept thy word," (Psa 119:67). I knew that the things I had to forfeit were foolish and vain but they had been deeply entwined in my identity since I was a little child. Only God could kill them and my cooperation was definitely needed. The water that flowed into the cylinder in the dream must have represented the cleansing water of God's Word. So this is my testimony of the most recent working of God in my life to conquer in me the vanity and pride that would not be permitted in his kingdom. How much longer till I become a worm? Only God knows.

Verse and Interpretation

Rev 6:2 And I saw, and behold a white horse: and he that sat on him had a bow; and a crown was given unto him:

and he went forth conquering, and to conquer.

I understood that my spiritual body had been awakened (I saw and behold a white horse). I also understood that Jesus who had come to me in this way was going to do a deeper work in my life to make me into the simplest fabric so he could form me into a perfect human being (and he that sat on him had a bow). I had given him authority over my life to do this (a crown was given unto him), and he was coming to conquer everything in me of my sinful nature that kept me from being able to enter his kingdom (he went forth conquering and to conquer).

Chapter Nine

The Red and Black Horses

Rev 6:3, 4 And when he had opened the second seal, I heard the second beast say, Come and see. And there went out another horse that was red: and power was given to him that sat thereon to take peace from the earth, and that they should kill one another: and there was given unto him a great sword.

The predominant word in verse 3 is "second." "Two" is the number of division and difference. This is the second seal, a different understanding opened that was not understood before. This is a different (second) body (beast) and division (two) is taking place. We will better understand the meaning of the red horse and the division taking place by seeing exactly what Bullinger wrote regarding the number two:

> We now come to the spiritual significance of the number Two. We have seen that *One* excludes all difference, and denotes that which is sovereign. But Two affirms that there is a difference—there is *another*; while One affirms that there is not another! ...It is the first number by which we can *divide* another, and therefore in all its uses we may trace this fundamental idea of *division* or *difference*.

In verse one we saw that the beast represents our body. Our body is speaking to us as happens when Jesus comes to us and awakens our spiritual body. We learned that the white horse represents our spiritual body upon which the Lord rests. The red horse represents a different body within our body, this being the physical body with which we interact with our physical earth. This horse is red, the color of our blood that supplies life to all the cells of our body. This body has certain needs that must be satisfied if its life is to continue in this physical world. It must have food and water, sleep, shelter, clothing, a comfortable temperature and it must procreate. Concerns over getting these needs met can take away our peace. People will kill others to get these needs met. So we can see that this body is very different from the first body because it has a dependence upon the physical world.

When the Lord comes and awakens the spiritual body, one of the first things he does after this is to divide the spiritual body from the physical body. I know this for two reasons: (1) I have experienced this, and (2) many places in Scripture relate this but it is mostly hidden in types. The most obvious place that is not hidden in a type is found in Hebrews 4:12 "For the word of God is quick, and powerful, and sharper than any two-edged sword, piercing even to the dividing asunder of soul and spirit, and of the joints and marrow, and is a discerner of the thoughts and intents of the heart."

At this point I would like to quote from Watchman Nee in Volume One of his three volume work entitled, *The Spiritual Man*. He begins the following paragraph by commenting on a scripture in 1 Thessalonians that says we are comprised of three parts. "And the very God of peace sanctify you wholly; and I pray God your whole spirit and soul and body be preserved blameless unto the coming of our Lord Jesus Christ" (1 Th 5:23). He then goes on to say that God will divide those parts:

> Not only does 1 Thessalonians divide man into three parts; other passages in the Scripture do the same. Hebrews 4:12 says, "For the word of God is living and operative and sharper than any two-edged sword, and piercing even to the dividing of soul and spirit and of joints and marrow, and able to discern the thoughts and intentions of the heart." Here the apostle divided the non-physical elements of man into two parts, the soul and the spirit, and he considered the physical part of man to include the joints and the marrow which correspond to the mind and the will. Just as a priest divided up a whole sacrifice and cut it apart with a knife so that nothing remained hidden, in the same way the Lord Jesus divides those who belong to Him, through the word of God. He pierces and divides every part, whether it be the spiritual, the soulish, or the physical. Since the soul and the spirit can be divided, the two must not be the same thing. Hence, this portion of the Word also considers man to be composed of three elements: the spirit, the soul, and the body.

When Nee writes that the Lord divides the physical part of man he likens the joints and marrow to the mind and the will. That was all he could surmise at the time of this writing during his life on this earth because it was not yet time for humankind to understand or experience the separating of the bodies. I believe the mind and the will which Nee likened to parts of the physical body are actually parts of the soul or the spirit. The joints and the marrow are definitely parts of the physical body and the Lord does indeed divide our bodies as I am explaining here in this chapter of Revelation.

My Experience

I said earlier that one reason I know the Lord divides the spiritual body from the natural body is that I have experienced it. Shortly after the awakening of my spiritual body, I began to feel something tingly moving up and down in the center of the entire trunk of my body. From the lower part of my abdomen up to my throat I felt this constant movement. It was almost like the flickering movement of a flame but it was not hot. It is difficult to explain something so spiritual in human words. There was absolutely no pain—only the knowledge that God was at work in my body. This feeling was constant and continued for a few days. Everywhere I went and no matter what I was doing, I felt this constant activity of tingling, flame-like movement vertically moving up and down the very center of the trunk of my body. I knew the Lord was separating my spiritual body from my natural body. I knew this because of my daily, in-depth studies of the Word and by the understanding imparted to me by the Holy Spirit.

Why the Separation?

God separates the spiritual body from the natural body to begin the process of this mortal putting on immortality. He works on the bodies separately according to his plan for each body as it pertains to coming into perfection. Immediately after the separation, the spiritual body is immature in that the feeling of God's presence is very faint although definitely perceptible. Over time as the spiritual body matures, the feeling of God's presence grows much stronger. The natural body needs to be purified and prepared for further separation from the body of sin and the body of death. If the physical body is to survive the disasters of nuclear war, nuclear reactor disasters, the pollution of our food, water and air, etc., it must be free of the weaknesses that came on it at the Fall in the form of sin and death. These must be separated out. Once this is accomplished, God will bring together the matured spiritual body with the purified physical body and this mortal will have put on immortality.

We see this process hidden in allegorical types in the Old Testament. The first that comes to mind is the account of Abram in Genesis 15 where God initiates a covenant with him promising that his progeny will enter the Promised Land:

> And he brought him forth abroad, and said, Look now toward heaven, and tell the stars, if thou be able to number them: and he said unto him, So shall thy seed be. And he believed in the LORD; and he counted it to him for righteousness. And he said unto him, I am the LORD that brought thee out of Ur of the Chaldees, to give thee this land to inherit it. And he said, Lord GOD, whereby shall I know that I shall inherit it? And he said unto him, Take me an heifer of three years old, and a she goat of three years old, and a ram of three years old, and a turtledove, and a young pigeon. And he took unto him all these, and divided them in the midst, and laid each piece one against another: but the birds divided he not. And when the fowls came down upon the carcases, Abram drove them away. And when the sun was going down, a deep sleep fell upon Abram; and, lo, an horror of great darkness fell upon him. And he said unto Abram, Know of a surety that thy seed shall be a stranger in a land that is not theirs, and shall serve them; and they shall afflict them four hundred years; And also that nation, whom they shall serve, will I judge: and afterward shall they come out with great substance. And thou shalt go to

thy fathers in peace; thou shalt be buried in a good old age. But in the fourth generation they shall come hither again: for the iniquity of the Amorites is not yet full. And it came to pass, that, when the sun went down, and it was dark, behold a smoking furnace, and a burning lamp that passed between those pieces (Gen 15:5-17).

In Genesis 15, God showed Abram the stars in the heavens and said, "So shall thy seed be." His seed is Christ (Gal 3:16). We who belong to Christ are as the stars of the heavens. When we receive our inheritance of a glorified body free from all sickness, aging and death, we will shine forth as the stars in the heavens as prophesied in Dan. 12:3, "And they that be wise shall shine as the brightness of the firmament; and they that turn many to righteousness as the stars forever and ever."

Abram asked God, "How shall I know that I shall inherit it?" Then God gave him instructions that reveal allegorically something of what God will do in us when it is time for us to fully take our inheritance here on earth. It has to do with the process we will go through as we come into perfection in the end times. Abram took the bodies of three different animals, each three years of age, and divided them in the middle at the word of the Lord. These would represent the physical body being divided—those parts that become part of the glorified body separated from the parts of mortality to be discarded. Then he took two birds, a turtledove and a young pigeon, but these he did not divide (higher bodies meaning spiritual bodies). "And it came to pass, that, when the sun went down, and it was dark, behold a smoking furnace, and a burning lamp that passed between those pieces."

We are living in the end of the age (when the sun went

down). There is great darkness of terrible evil coming upon the earth (and it was dark). God is separating the parts of our bodies, the sin from the natural body and the natural body from the spiritual body, by the smoking furnace that burns out all sin nature and the burning lamp (*lappiyd*) of full salvation that passes between the parts. We are the descendants of Abram that are entering in to possess the land. The birds that were not cut in half represent the spiritual (heavenly) body because birds fly in the heavenly realm. The spiritual body will be separated from the physical body but the spiritual body itself will not have to be divided.

Another place where we see the separating of the bodies is in Ezekiel 1:13:

> Ezek 1:13 As for the likeness of the living creatures, their appearance was like burning coals of fire, and like the appearance of lamps: it went up and down among the living creatures; and the fire was bright, and out of the fire went forth lightning.

Without going into detail here (which would be difficult because the interpretation of this verse is based on the preceding twelve verses) I will give a brief explanation. The living creatures are God's people in the end times who are in the process of coming into the fullness of Christ. The number four is not to be taken literally but only for its spiritual meaning which is "man in relation to the earth as created" (Bullinger). The appearance of burning coals and lamps that went up and down among the creatures is speaking of the separating of the physical body from the spiritual body happening in each individual. The rest of Ezekiel One details how God works in the bodies, divides out what is not to be kept, and then eventually brings them together.

There are other places where this process can be seen allegorically. One is in the breaking of the pitchers in the account of Gideon and another is regarding Sampson and the setting on fire of torches tied to the tails of foxes. For those interested in doing deeper study, these are good places to start. It is also found in the tabernacle regarding the curtains (spiritual body) and the goats' hair curtains (natural body).

Getting back to Revelation 6:4, we read that to the one sitting on the red horse there was given a great sword. This Greek word for "given" can also be translated as "received." So we could also say that the one sitting on the red horse received a great sword. The great sword would be the word of God wielded by none other than the Word Himself. This is the great sword of Heb 4:12 "For the word of God is quick, and powerful, and sharper than any two-edged sword, piercing even to the dividing asunder of soul and spirit, and of the joints and marrow, and is a discerner of the thoughts and intents of the heart." When I felt the separating of my spiritual body from my physical body I was feeling this great sword being wielded by Jesus. In this way I received the sword.

Verse and Interpretation

Rev 6:3, 4 And when he had opened the second seal, I heard the second beast say, Come and see. And there went out another horse that was red: and power was given to him that sat thereon to take peace from the earth, and that they should kill one another: and there was given unto him a great sword.

When Jesus opened my understanding again (opened the second seal) I felt a different message in my body (second beast say, Come and see). This message was about division and difference regarding my bodies. I knew I had a body that was very different from my spiritual body. This other body was my natural body that had many needs and weaknesses (red horse) that often caused me to worry over whether or not my needs would be met (take peace from the earth.) I could feel that my natural body with all its needs and weakness was being separated from my spiritual body by a great sword in the hand of Jesus (given to him a great sword).

* * * * * * * * * * * * * * * *

Rev 6:5 And when he had opened the third seal, I heard the third beast say, Come and see. And I beheld, and lo a black horse; and he that sat on him had a pair of balances in his hand.

Jesus opens the third seal to give me an understanding about something that I had not known before. This new understanding comes through my body because it is still a beast that is saying, Come and see. This is the third seal and the third beast. Three is the number which stands for completion and divine perfection. Therefore, this new understanding coming from my body is something that will cause me to come to completion and perfection.

Since this is a black horse, we know this is not something good because black is associated with evil and the absence of God and his light. However, knowing that in

Christ all things have a purpose this must be something that will be used in the process of coming into perfection and completion (three). A pair of balances must have to do with justice or judgment. As we come into perfection and completion, every deed and every thought must be weighed in the balances of God's perfect judgment.

I can explain this in terms of my experience. After my spiritual body was awakened (first beast) and after I felt the separating of my spiritual body from my natural body (second beast), I had a new understanding that came to me through my body (third beast/black horse). I came to realize that whenever I had a sinful or disobedient thought or action (black), the Lord would cause something unpleasant to manifest in my body as a signal to me that (1) something was wrong for which I needed to repent, and (2) as an incentive to not do again what I had just done (pair of balances).

This has been very much like a parent disciplining a child. I don't get by with anything. If I do what I know I am not supposed to do and I repent of my actions, I still suffer a consequence in my body. A recent example comes to mind. My husband and I had lunch at Applebee's. We ordered the "two for twenty" deal which comes with an appetizer. He chose French fried onion rings. I knew I wasn't supposed to eat them because they are fried in oil that is genetically modified and the Lord wants me to avoid that kind of food. I struggled with the temptation for awhile but then came up with some sort of rationalization that it was probably all right—after all I didn't order them and they were part of the meal. I ate two. Shortly thereafter I felt as though I had a grain of sand under one eyelid. I was shopping at Wal-Mart feeling absolutely miserable because of that eye. I repented of eating the onion rings but the unpleasant feeling continued until I finished shopping and then it left just as quickly as it had come. The next time I'm faced with a similar situation, I will probably resist the temptation. How do I know the eye irritation was chastisement from God? If the same thing happens several times under similar circumstances then you know it is the Lord's discipline. There are certain things in my life that have occurred repeatedly over a period of several years that I know are the direct result of my disobedience.

Sometimes there can be a good reward for not succumbing to temptation. One day several years ago I was shopping in K-Mart. I was tempted to buy a teeth whitening kit. (This had to do with my concerns over what other people think of me and was therefore probably not allowed although the Lord had never said specifically that I could not whiten my teeth.) I spent considerable time looking at different options. They all seemed expensive to me and I finally decided not to buy one. I went on with my shopping and just as I paid the cashier and gathered up my purchases to leave, I felt the Lord patting the top of my head. I knew he was rewarding me for not buying the item in question. As for having white teeth, the Lord had another plan. I have not been allowed to drink coffee or wine for many years now. That took care of the stained teeth problem!

God truly is a perfect parent who means what he says and always follows through on the consequences he has warned us about—and he doesn't count to three before administering his discipline! I recently had an experience that demonstrates how strict the Lord is in expecting our full compliance with his instructions.

We were spending a week with our daughter and her family in Indiana. It was Christmas day and we were all seated around the table loading up our plates with the delicious turkey dinner my daughter and I had spent several hours preparing. As I put the first few items on my plate, I felt a strong tickle in my nose. It was the kind of feeling that precedes a sneeze and I recognized that as being a signal from the Lord that I was about to do something wrong. I had no idea what it could be so I continued on with my dinner.

As I was eating I was questioning the Lord in my mind. I was trying to think what I was doing at the very moment my nose tickled. It came to me that I was putting gravy on my food at that moment. Then it slowly dawned on me what the problem was. I had made the gravy and the only thickener my daughter had on hand was cornstarch, so I used that. I am not allowed to eat any grains. At home I thicken sauces with arrowroot which is not a grain. That is what the Lord had warned me about. It made no difference that I didn't know at the time why I was being warned. I still had to endure my consequence. Then the next day when we had leftovers for dinner, I totally forgot and put gravy on my food again. Again I had to bear my consequence which was something unpleasant in my body.

God is not unreasonable. If there was nothing to eat but something with grains, I could eat it and not be disciplined. For example, we were recently invited to dinner at the home of some friends where dinner consisted of lasagna and green salad. I could not refuse the lasagna as there was nothing else. That was permitted. At the Christmas turkey dinner described above, I did not have to eat the gravy. There was plenty of other food that was permitted. In that case, when the warning came I should have simply waited a little until I understood instead of continuing on after just a second of reflection.

With the black horse, God's warning comes through our body and our consequence for disobedience comes through our body also. A warning could take any form such as a tickle in the nose, a sneeze, an itchy eye, a jab of tooth pain, sudden vertigo or just anything that catches our attention and is not particularly pleasant. The consequence can take any form according to however God chooses to work in our body. The Lord is always loving and kind with no anger or retribution whatsoever, but he cannot be manipulated or cajoled.

If the Lord's instructions seem too detailed or nitpicking I assure you they are not. He is preparing us for ministry in the end times. This will be a ministry of great power. God can only entrust his power to those whom he knows of a certainty will only use it according to his direction and will. There is nothing on earth or in this universe as important as becoming like Christ, and this is the way God has chosen to do it. In the process we get to learn more about God's character and ways. His closeness and attention to the minutest detail of our lives is astounding. He truly does know our thoughts and every word on our tongue before we speak it.

Verse and Interpretation

Rev 6:5 And when he had opened the third seal, I heard the third beast say, Come and see. And I beheld, and lo a black horse; and he that sat on him had a pair of balances in his hand.

And when Jesus opened my understanding about how I would come into completion and divine perfection (opened the third seal) the understanding came in the form of messages received from my body (heard the third beast say, Come and see). I began to feel unpleasant things in my body (black horse) that were in direct correlation to my disobedience to God (he that sat on him had a pair of balances in his hand).

* * * * * * * * * * * * * * * *

Rev 6:6 And I heard a voice in the midst of the four beasts say, A measure of wheat for a penny, and three measures of barley for a penny; and see thou hurt not the oil and the wine.

Here again God speaks to me from the midst of my body (four beasts). God says there are going to be limitations set on your life (a measure of wheat for a penny, etc). This message comes in the way I described in the previous verse's interpretation. Over time on a daily basis God makes known to us what is permissible and what is not.

Here in verse six God uses some things from natural life as an example—wheat and barley. If wheat and barley were free, a person would naturally take all they could get into their shopping cart and come back for more. But there is a limitation in that you can only have as much as you can afford. Most people have only a certain amount of money they can spend on food. Therefore, they are limited in how much they can take. In Matthew 20, a penny was a full day's wage, so this would definitely limit how much a person could have.

The Lord places limitations on many areas of our lives at this stage of our conformity to the image of Christ. Food is a big part of our lives and I have found there to be many restrictions in this area. His limitations were placed on me gradually so I would be able to comply. The Lord didn't start with me by saying, Don't eat sugar. He began by saying, Don't eat that little bowl of chocolate chips you have every night after dinner. Then it was, You may have dessert once a week. Then it was allowable only with friends for a special occasion. Gradually I eliminated all foods containing sugar. Some of these were not mandatory. If I felt I just had to have a few sweet pickles with my lunch, I could, but he let me know that it would slightly lessen my ability to feel his presence.

These food-related limitations not only make our body healthier but they also crucify the flesh. We cannot enter the Kingdom without being disciplined in our natural life. It is part of taking up our cross: "If any man will come after me, let him deny himself, and take up his cross daily, and follow me" (Luke 9:23).

Food is not the only thing in my life God has placed limitations on. There have been other things to which the Lord has assigned specific restrictions or conditions. I am not permitted to watch television at all. It makes no difference how good the program might be, I'm not allowed to watch it—not even for a minute. Again, this restriction was not placed on me all of a sudden but gradually over time. The Lord has given specific guidelines regarding sleep, daily exercise, daily worship and just about everything else in my life. I want to assure you that these restrictions are not onerous because they crucify more of my flesh which in turn allows for a greater intensity of feeling the Lord's presence—and that is worth any restriction!

The Oil and the Wine

We have seen (regarding the wheat and the barley) that the Lord imposes certain restrictions on our lives when he is working in us to conform us to the image of his Son. There are other things in this verse that are to be without restriction. These are the things of the Spirit as allegorically seen in the oil and the wine. Oil is often a symbol of the Holy Spirit; wine is also symbolic in that it represents the good things of God's Spirit, more specifically love and faith. We are to have the Holy Spirit with his love and faith without limitations. If we were to close our life to this, it would grieve (hurt) the Holy Spirit (oil and wine). "And grieve not the holy Spirit of God, whereby ye are sealed unto the day of redemption." This is what the scripture is saying in "hurt not the oil and the wine."

If we are not watching television or engaged in worldly activities we are going to find we have much more time for God. He wants us to talk to him about everything and study his Word as much as possible. Then we are to minister by God's Spirit to others in the body. In this way we will not harm the wine or the oil. They will increase in us.

Verse and Interpretation

Rev 6:6 And I heard a voice in the midst of the four beasts say, A measure of wheat for a penny, and three measures of barley for a penny; and see thou hurt not the oil and the wine.

I heard God speak to me (I heard a voice) through my

body (midst of the four beasts) placing limitations on what I was permitted to do in all areas of my life (a measure of wheat for a penny, and three measures of barley for a penny); there were no limitations placed on anything I did pertaining to the things of the Holy Spirit (hurt not the oil and the wine.

Chapter Ten
Death Comes to Death

Rev 6:7 And when he had opened the fourth seal, I heard the voice of the fourth beast say, Come and see.

Knowing the spiritual meaning of "four" for fourth seal and fourth beast will help unlock the meaning of this verse. According to Bullinger four is the number of creation, of man in his relation to all that is created. It is the number of the world, and it represents man's weakness, and helplessness, and vanity.

In this verse Jesus again opened to me an understanding about my body that had been unknown to me. This understanding came from my body (fourth beast) and it had to do with my own weakness, helplessness and vanity (four). We all know that our bodies possess elements of weakness and helplessness and that they eventually die, but here I am learning something regarding this I could not know or experience until the fourth seal was opened. So with the opening of this seal I am now released to understand something about my body that had been shut away from me—something inaccessible to me because it was sealed. Only Jesus could do this thing in me. If Jesus does it, it has to be good. When looking at the fourth seal and the fourth horse literally and outwardly, it looks bad, but this has to be good because Jesus is doing this thing in our body (fourth beast). We look to the next verse to see what this good thing is that Jesus is doing.

Verse and Interpretation

Rev 6:7 And when he had opened the fourth seal, I heard the voice of the fourth beast say, Come and see.

Jesus opened my understanding about something having to do with the weakness, helplessness and vanity (fourth) of my body (beast).

* * * * * * * * * * * * * * *

Rev 6:8 And I looked, and behold a pale horse: and his name that sat on him was Death, and Hell followed with him. And power was given unto them over the fourth part of the earth, to kill with sword, and with hunger, and with death, and with the beasts of the earth.

The Greek word for pale is *chloros* from which we derive the word "chlorophyll." It occurs four times in Scripture and is translated "green" everywhere but here. Twice it is green grass and once it is green thing. So this could just as well have been translated "Behold a green horse." I suppose that because we associate green with living things and this verse appears to be about death, the word pale was chosen by translators rather than green. This choice has helped to keep the true meaning of this verse hidden until it was time for the church of the end times to understand the mystery hidden behind this seal.

We have seen in the first three horses that the horse represents something having to do with our body. Therefore a pale horse is also about our body. This is an aspect of our body that is green and of the earth with the characteristics of helplessness, weakness and vanity. All green and living things on this earth eventually die so we see from this fact, as well as from the words of Scripture here, that Death rides on this horse. This means that this aspect of our body is going to die. Not our body itself but this condition of our body will die. In other words, the creatureliness of our body, the part of our body that causes us to eventually grow old and weak and die will no longer exist. Jesus is going to remove this part of our body. This has to take place in order for this mortal to put on immortality.

Not only does the horse represent our body but so does earth. Our bodies came from the earth (Gen 2:7) and that is where they return upon death. However in this verse the seal of death has been opened and there will be no more death because the only part of us that can die is the "fourth part of the earth" with fourth being the part of our body (earth) that has always been subject to death.

This verse says that "power was given unto them over the fourth part of the earth." At first look it would seem that this was granting to Death something it had not had before. However, Death has always taken the life of every living thing on earth. To only be able to kill a fourth part of the earth (with earth being the human body [four beasts]) would actually be placing a limitation on Death. The only part of us he can kill is our human frailty.

How is my body (fourth beast) saying to me that I'm not going to die (Come and see)? I have new strength and vitality in my body. My outward appearance does not look any different, but the stamina and vitality I have is beyond anything I have known. I see this in the fact that I only need about half as much sleep as I used to, and even though I am sleeping less, I have more energy. My body is stronger to withstand flu, colds and that sort of thing. I'm not coming down with the chronic diseases most people expect to get as they age.

I have believed since 1972 that I, as well as many others, will not die. There have been many times God has confirmed this to me personally, and there are Scriptures that plainly say that at some point in time, death will no longer have power over God's people.

In 1Corinthians 15 Paul writes at length about our bodies. He contrasts the natural body with the spiritual body as he says:

> … There is a natural body, and there is a spiritual body. And so it is written, the first man Adam was made a living soul; the last Adam was made a quickening spirit. Howbeit that was not first which is spiritual, but that which is natural; and afterward that which is spiritual. The first man is of the earth, earthy: the second man is the Lord from heaven. As is the earthy, such are they also that are earthy: and as is the heavenly, such are they also that are heavenly. And as we have borne the image of the earthy, we shall also bear the image of the heavenly (1 Cor 15:44b – 49).

Here in Paul's explanation of the two bodies, he uses the terms earthy and heavenly. With the pale horse we see that what dies is that in us that is earthy. This is the fourth part of the earth.

There have been a few times when the Lord showed me something in a dream that related to the particular Bible study I was doing. A few years ago as I was writing about this concept of the bodies in *The Four Living Creatures*, I had the following dream that helped me understand the separation of the two bodies and the removal of mortality from the physical body. Here is what I wrote in that book:

> In this dream my mother gave me a family heirloom—a coffee table that on the underneath side had the signatures of all my grandmothers from ages past. The coffee table had two levels that were connected one to the other on each side by some sort of hinge device that held them about six inches apart yet gave them mobility in that they could move back and forth independent of each other. At one point I saw myself holding one half of one level in my hands. I looked at the coffee table and it looked complete yet I had one half of one level in my hands that had been cut straight down the middle.
>
> As I prayed for the interpretation of the dream, God revealed that the coffee table represented my natural and spiritual bodies as inherited from my ancestors. The bodies were separate yet connected and mobile. The half I held in my hands was the portion representing mortality that God had severed and removed. The coffee table was now complete but immortality had replaced the place where mortality had dwelt (from *The Four Living Creatures*).

Years later as I write about the four horses and reflect back on this dream I find it interesting that the portion of the coffee table I was holding in my hands was one fourth. This ties in perfectly with my interpretation of the pale horse as Death destroying one fourth of the body. That, of course, would be the part of the coffee table that had been removed and I was holding in my hands.

A few days after I had this dream, my husband had a dream that showed the same principle in a different way. He dreamed he was going to be operated on. The bottom half of his body was going to be removed and he was getting a new half. In the dream he was happy about having the operation—like there was no fear, only delightful anticipation. I believe the bottom half represented the mortality in his body that was going to be replaced with immortality.

Getting back to the passage in 1 Corinthians about our two bodies, Paul goes on to explain that there will come a time when death will no longer be able to claim our bodies:

> Behold, I show you a mystery; We shall not all sleep, but we shall all be changed, in a moment, in the twinkling of an eye, at the last trump: for the trumpet shall sound, and the dead shall be raised incorruptible, and we shall be changed. For this corruptible must put on incorruption, and this mortal must put on immortality. So when this corruptible shall have put on incorruption, and this mortal shall have put on immortality, then shall be brought to pass the saying that is written, Death is swallowed up in victory (1 Cor 15:51-54).

Now I would like to apply this passage to our understanding of the last part of Rev 6: 8, "to kill with sword, and with hunger, and with death, and with the beasts of the earth." This is how the fourth part of the earth, the part of our body that has made us susceptible to death, will die. The very principle of death in our body will itself die! Since I have not experienced this yet, I can only explain this based on my knowledge of Scripture which should suffice for now. There are four ways listed here that the death principle in us will die. Let's look at each of these one by one:

The Sword

I see this as a reference to the sword of Heb 4:12." For the word of God is quick, and powerful, and sharper than any two-edged sword, piercing even to the dividing asunder of soul and spirit, and of the joints and marrow, and is a discerner of the thoughts and intents of the heart." For us to enter into immortality with a body that is incorruptible there must be separation. The parts must be separated for a time so God can do his work; hence the need for the work of the sword. Jesus, himself, is the Word. The Bible is the Word. Only Jesus can do this work of separating the body of death from the rest of the body in order for it to be killed. He needs our cooperation in that we must remain in the Word that our spirit can be nourished on a daily basis.

It is interesting to note the verses directly preceding Heb 4:12 that speak of our need to enter into the Lord's rest. Even as God rested on the seventh day of creation, we too are to enter into this same rest. We will only enter this rest when God's work in us is completed and we have been perfected. This is not a rest where we just sit around and do nothing. This is a rest where we will be busier than we have ever been. How can this be? It is because God will be ministering and working through us. We will not labor to preach, teach, heal, cast out demons, raise the dead or countless other functions of the Holy Spirit. God will do it all through us as we rest in him and just love and enjoy him. What a rest this will be! And this rest will only come as we are separated by the sword of the Lord and death does its work in us.

It is through death that we are delivered and perfected. It was through death that Jesus defeated the Devil: "Forasmuch then as the children are partakers of flesh and blood, he also himself likewise took part of the same; that through death he might destroy him that had the power of death, that is, the devil; And deliver them who through fear of death were all their lifetime subject to bondage" (Heb 2:14, 15). Our coming into completion in the end times will be accomplished by our own death to self and then by the death of the principle of physical death that indwells the members of our body. It is the sword of the Lord that will accomplish this in us.

Hunger

Only God can destroy the principle of death (the body of death) in us, but we have our part to do. We must starve it according to the leading of the Holy Spirit. We all have a tendency to like food that harms our body, and yet we sometimes eat it anyway. Some of us eat it every day knowing we are harming our health, but we just can't seem to say No. Unhealthy foods are the most readily available, least expensive and tasty even though they are laden with sugar, fat, salt, damaging chemicals such as monosodium glutamate, preservatives, fillers and dyes. People who indulge in these foods have more health problems than people who don't. I can only conclude that these foods feed the death principle in us and we should avoid them.

Avoiding unhealthy food is becoming increasingly difficult and more expensive because of the greed and vice that controls the food industry which is owned by as few as ten companies in the U.S. Their strong lobby in Congress favors the passage of laws that consistently militate against the health of the American people. Laws have recently been passed to enable food manufacturers and distributors to sell genetically engineered foods without having to label them as such. There are several foreign countries who refuse to buy certain foods grown in the U.S. because they are genetically modified. These countries do more to protect their people than the American government does to protect their own citizens.

God will help us starve the death principle by telling us specifically what we are allowed or not allowed to eat. When the spiritual body has been awakened and we can feel God speaking to us through our body, there is no difficulty in knowing what he is saying. I am often amazed at how clearly he speaks and how intimately acquainted with every detail of my life he is. There are three major food restrictions he has placed on me and these are no sugar, no grains, and drink only water. Grains were freely eaten in the biblical times but grains today are different. Most today are genetically modified and grown with liberal pesticide use. As I struggled with not having bread or pastry of any sort, I learned that there are many kinds of flour I had never heard of—flours made from seeds, nuts, beans and other things. I learned to make my own bread using five different flours. As for water, we live in a remote area where we get water from our own deep well. When we travel by car, I take my own water and much of my own food with us. One day as I was reading 1Tim 4:3-5, the Lord impressed upon me that when no good food options are available, if we will pray and ask God to sanctify the food to our use, he will do it.

Death

When death is swallowed up in victory, death itself will

have died. Most of Romans 8 reveals that we will overcome death in the end times. I will take just a few passages from that exciting chapter to quote here:

> And if Christ be in you, the body is dead because of sin; but the Spirit is life because of righteousness. But if the Spirit of him that raised up Jesus from the dead dwell in you, he that raised up Christ from the dead shall also quicken your mortal bodies by his Spirit that dwelleth in you (Rom 8:10, 11).

> For if ye live after the flesh, ye shall die: but if ye through the Spirit do mortify the deeds of the body, ye shall live (Rom 8:13).

> For I reckon that the sufferings of this present time are not worthy to be compared with the glory which shall be revealed in us. For the earnest expectation of the creature waiteth for the manifestation of the sons of God. For the creature was made subject to vanity *("mataiotes" meaning fig. transientness)*, not willingly, but by reason of him who hath subjected the same in hope, because the creature itself also shall be delivered from the bondage of corruption into the glorious liberty of the children of God (Rom 8:18-21). (Italics mine.)

> Rom 8:23 And not only they, but ourselves also, which have the firstfruits of the Spirit, even we ourselves groan within ourselves, waiting for the adoption, to wit, the redemption of our body.

There are many places in the Bible indicating that at the return of Christ there will be great judgment on the wicked, but the righteous will inherit great blessings and eternal life.

One of those blessings will be the abolishment of death.

Beasts of the Earth

There are two places in the New Testament that say death will be swallowed up:

> So when this corruptible shall have put on incorruption, and this mortal shall have put on immortality, then shall be brought to pass the saying that is written, Death is swallowed up in victory (1 Cor 15:54).

> For we that are in this tabernacle do groan, being burdened: not for that we would be unclothed, but clothed upon, that mortality might be swallowed up of life (2 Cor 5:4).

Death is what will be killed by the beasts of the field, and this is, of course, figurative language. Have you ever seen a documentary about some place like Africa where an animal has made a kill and is now eating its prey? Perhaps you have seen it in person. It appears that they hardly even chew the flesh. They tear it off and swallow it whole. Or you may have seen a documentary where a snake swallows a small animal whole. To me this is a picture of how death will die. It will be swallowed up by life. There will be no escape for death.

Jesus said, "I am the way, the truth, and the life." Jesus conquered death for us and he will make it a reality in our lives physically when we experience death being swallowed up by life. Thinking back to what we learned regarding the white horse where Jesus comes to us conquering and to conquer, we can see here that one thing he will conquer in us is death.

The Holy Spirit has shown us here in Revelation 6:8 just how death is going to be destroyed at the time of the second coming of Christ.

1. The sword – The body of death will be separated out from the natural body.
2. Hunger – The body of death will be starved as we deprive it of what it desires.
3. Death – Death itself will die.
4. Beasts of the earth – Death will be swallowed up by life.

Verse and Interpretation

Rev 6:8 And I looked, and behold a pale horse: and his name that sat on him was Death, and Hell followed with him. And power was given unto them over the fourth part of the earth, to kill with sword, and with hunger, and with death, and with the beasts of the earth.

After Jesus opened the fourth seal, I saw a part of my body that was subject to weakness, helplessness and vanity (pale horse). This is what would cause me to die and go to the grave (his name that sat on him was Death and Hell followed with him). However, the power of death had been limited in that he could only kill the condition in me of weakness, helplessness and vanity (fourth part of the earth) and nothing else. This death would be accomplished by the Word of God (Jesus) separating this weak part out from the rest of my body as in Heb 4:12 (the sword). My part was to cooperate with God by obeying instructions that would lead to the starvation of this condition of weakness (with hunger). Then death itself would die (and with death) as mortality was swallowed up by life (beasts of the earth).

* *

Before continuing on to the next verse, I think a short review of what we have seen inwardly in the previous verses would be beneficial because all this needs to be understood contextually.

Summary Thus Far

The four horses represent four aspects of our body that correspond to the four bodies mentioned in New Testament Scripture—the spiritual body (1 Cor 15), the natural body (1 Cor 15), the body of sin (Rom 6) and the body of death (Rom 7).

The White Horse

I realized that Jesus (Lamb) had come to me and opened something within me that had been sealed off from me (one of the seals). This new thing opened to me was the slow, continuous and gentle movement of my spiritual body (noise of thunder) that was within my natural body (four beasts). This new experience was communicating something to me (come and see).

When I understood that my spiritual body had been awakened (I saw and behold a white horse), I also knew that Jesus, who had come to me in this way, was going to do a deeper work in my life to make me into the simplest fabric so he could form me into a perfect human being (and he that sat on him had a bow). I had given him authority over my life to do this (a crown was given unto him), and he was coming to conquer everything in me of my sinful nature that kept me from being able to enter his kingdom (he went forth conquering and to conquer).

The Red Horse

When Jesus opened my understanding again (opened the second seal) I felt a different message in my body (second beast say, Come and see). This message was about division and difference regarding my bodies. I knew I had a body that was very different from my spiritual body. This other body was my natural body that had many needs and weaknesses (red horse) that often caused me to worry over whether or not my needs would be met (take peace from the earth.) I could feel that my natural body with all its needs and weakness was being separated from my spiritual body by a great sword in the hand of Jesus (given to him a great sword).

The Black Horse

And when Jesus opened my understanding about how I would come into completion and divine perfection (opened the third seal) the understanding came in the form of messages received from my body (heard the third beast say, Come and see). I began to feel unpleasant things in my body (black horse) that were in direct correlation to my disobedience to God (he that sat on him had a pair of balances in his hand).

I heard God speak to me (I heard a voice) through my body (midst of the four beasts) placing limitations on what I was permitted to do in all areas of my life (a measure of wheat for a penny, and three measures of barley for a penny); there were no limitations placed on anything I did pertaining to the things of the Holy Spirit (hurt not the oil and the wine).

The Pale Horse

Jesus opened my understanding about something having to do with the weakness, helplessness and vanity (fourth) of my body (beast). After Jesus opened the fourth seal, I saw a part of my body that was subject to weakness, helplessness and vanity (pale horse). This is what would cause me to die and go to the grave (his name that sat on him was Death and Hell followed with him). However, the power of death had been limited in that he could only kill the condition in me of weakness, helplessness and vanity (fourth part of the earth) and nothing else. This death would be accomplished by the Word of God (Jesus) separating this weak part out from the rest of my body as in Heb 4:12 (the sword). My part was to cooperate with God by obeying instructions that would lead to the starvation of this condition of weakness (with hunger). Then death itself would die (and with death) as mortality was swallowed up by life (beasts of the earth).

* * * * * * * * * * * * * * * * * * *

Rev 6:9 And when he had opened the fifth seal, I saw under the altar the souls of them that were slain for the word of God, and for the testimony which they held:

It is important to remember that this interpretation is still inward rather than outward. Therefore, what he sees with the fifth seal is something within himself. This is something Jesus is showing him. Our first clue as to what this is can be found in the number five.

We can again turn to Bullinger for a deeper understanding of five. Most Bible students know that five is the number of grace, of unmerited favor. Bullinger points out that 5 is 4 + 1 indicating God's divine favor added to our weakness. It is by God's divine favor that we are "justified freely by his grace through the redemption that is in Christ Jesus" (Rom 3:24). Hence five is the number of redemption.

In the usual outward interpretation, these are the souls of martyrs in heaven. However, for our inward interpretation these are parts of our own soul that have passed through the cross, died to self, and are now in the presence of God. We are all a work in progress. Sanctification is a process. Nothing in us gets into heaven that has not first gone through the cross. As we work through difficult situations in life, we make choices for or against God's Word. When we choose to obey God, we often suffer in some way that causes the death of our sin nature and purifies an aspect of our soul that is then prepared for heaven. That part of us has been sanctified.

It is through much tribulation that we enter the Kingdom of God. It is the difficulties in life that give us the opportunity to choose God's way which almost always calls for sacrifice on our part. This is how we mature in God. At the level of maturity seen here in Revelation 6, there are many parts of this person's soul that have been sanctified. There is a longing within him to move forward into perfection and immortality, but as the next verse reveals, they have to wait awhile longer because there are more parts of the person that still need to be purified.

We see these souls spiritually when we recognize that we are different now in many ways from what we used to be. Character defects we used to have are gone. We go through situations realizing that a work has been done. Something that would have upset us before no longer does. Things that used to cause fear, no longer do. There is peace, rest, joy, confidence and all manner of good qualities of Christ evident in our life. People around us see that we are different from others and from the way we used to be.

Verse and Interpretation

Rev 6:9 And when he had opened the fifth seal, I saw under the altar the souls of them that were slain for the word of God, and for the testimony which they held:

Jesus revealed to me something about the redemption of my soul (when he had opened the fifth seal). I could see that because of my willingness to obey his Word by following Jesus, denying myself and taking up my cross (slain for the word of God), I was different. My life had become a testimony for others to see how Jesus can change a person's life (for the testimony which they held).

* * * * * * * * * * * * * * *

Chapter Eleven

Waiting

Rev 6:10 And they cried with a loud voice, saying, How long, O Lord, holy and true, dost thou not judge and avenge our blood on them that dwell on the earth?

If we interpreted this outwardly and literally, these would be people who had died a violent martyr's death on earth who now want vengeance. Our inward interpretation, though, reveals something quite different. As explained above, these are the parts of our self that have died to self and are ready to enter fully into the Kingdom of Heaven. However, they can't go yet because there are still parts of their self (those that dwell on earth) that have yet to be purified by the work of the cross. Everything in our soul, no matter how good it may be, must go through the cross to be cleansed of impure, selfish motives before it can enter the Kingdom.

I think many Christians can identify with this—I know I do. I long to see Jesus face-to-face. I want to hear his voice. I do experience him in many ways, but I want more. It bothers me that I can still be so carnal in some respects when I have experienced so much of the liberation of the cross in other aspects of my life.

Many people may have difficulty understanding the

dividedness of the soul as I explain in these verses. However, I have literally seen this to be true as I've ministered one-on-one to severely abused people. There are people, many people, who have suffered extreme childhood abuse at the hands of others who used them in their efforts to gain power from the Devil. The abuse often begins at birth (or in the womb) and continues for a lifetime. The only way to survive this abuse and remain sane is to dissociate—to form alternate personality parts—and thereby separate their consciousness from the memory of the abuse. People who have suffered in this way have a lot of problems in life as a result of the abuse and yet, they may not remember it. They may seek help from mental health professionals who may label them as being schizophrenic, bipolar or some such diagnosis and prescribe drugs to hopefully help with their symptoms. However they can't truly heal them because only Jesus Christ can do that and prayer is often not believed in or even allowed in some mental health professional settings. Many of these abused persons look to the church for help. Many churches don't understand and send abused persons to the mental health professionals.

I have been blessed by a call of God on my life to help these individuals. I have, through prayer and the power of the Holy Spirit, been able to meet many of these dissociated parts and hear their memories. Once they have a memory, they are able to renounce the lies they believed because of the abuse and replace them with truth, forgive their tormenters and release their pain. Jesus ministers to them and then either merges them into the person or keeps them separated in a safe place inside until such time as they are mature enough to be integrated. The little child parts need to mature before they can be merged. Jesus takes them to a safe place in the person's spirit where they are nurtured and cared for until they are ready for integration. Many severely abused persons are open to a realm of Spirit that enables them to see this taking place within. People who have not been abused are not necessarily divided into different personalities. However, none of us is truly whole until we come through the process of sanctification.

Verse and Interpretation

Rev 6:10 And they cried with a loud voice, saying, How long, O Lord, holy and true, dost thou not judge and avenge our blood on them that dwell on the earth?

The parts of me that had experienced death to self eagerly desired to enter into the fullness of Christ. It was difficult to wait for other parts that were still dwelling in their carnal, earthly state to go through their death to self as well.

* * * * * * * * * * * * * * * * *

Rev 6:11 And white robes were given unto every one of them; and it was said unto them, that they should rest yet for a little season, until their fellowservants also and their brethren, that should be killed as they were, should be fulfilled.

As I explained above, severely abused persons are often able to see this process of sanctification taking place within as different dissociated parts go through purification. This takes place as they process through each abuse memory. With an understanding minister or layperson assisting, the lies they believed because of the abuse are replaced with truth, perpetrators are forgiven, bitter root judgments and vows are renounced, pain is released and, yes, demons are cast out. We do have to deal with demons in this ministry but that is not so difficult as some might think. Demons are in people because they have a legal right to be there—a legal right being lies believed, unforgiveness harbored, hatred, vows, etc. Once those are dealt with in ministry, demons have to leave...and they won't be back.

It is easy to see that when all the above has been accomplished in a part, that part is sanctified as all the sin has been cleared out. It is then ready to be merged into the main person or go to a safe place in the person's spirit where they wait for more of their self (fellow servants) to go through the process. In ministry for extreme abuse, the parts are ministered to individually as the Lord brings them forward. For those of us who were not abused, the situations we face in life can accomplish the same thing. Adversity has a way of bringing to the surface of our life anger, fear, hatred and all manner of evil that was lodged in our heart of which we were unaware. We learn in such situations to sort out lies from truth, forgive, identify and renounce judgments we have made, etc. As we go through this process, our brethren in the church should also be going through this process. God desires to move us forward together as we are his body, members one of another.

This verse says that white robes were given to every one of them. These robes are symbolic of the moral purity they now possess. This is sometimes literally seen by abused persons as I minister to them. For example, a woman may have processed through a memory of extreme physical and sexual abuse that left her feeling dirty and ashamed. After we pray through her memory as explained above, she sometimes sees Jesus or his angels wash her clean in a beautiful waterfall and then clothe her in a pretty white dress (white robe).

Verse and Interpretation

Rev 6:11 And white robes were given unto every one of them; and it was said unto them, that they should rest yet for a little season, until their fellowservants also and their brethren, that should be killed as they were, should be fulfilled.

The parts that were so eager to move into the fullness of Christ (previous verse) were comforted by God in knowing that even though they were fully sanctified (white robes) they should rest and enjoy their cleansed state for a little while longer (a little season) while they wait for the rest of their self (fellow servants) and their fellow Christians (brethren) to also come to the same state of purity (killed as they were).

* * * * * * * * * * * * * * *

Rev 6:12 And I beheld when he had opened the sixth seal, and, lo, there was a great earthquake; and the sun became black as sackcloth of hair, and the moon became as blood;

In the previous verse we saw the parts of this person that have been purified. Now this verse will tell us about the parts that have not been purified and how they will go through a sanctifying experience. The Lord tells about purification in preparation for his coming in Malachi:

> Mal 3:1 Behold, I will send my messenger, and he shall prepare the way before me: and the Lord, whom ye seek, shall suddenly come to his temple, even the messenger of the covenant, whom ye delight in: behold, he shall come, saith the LORD of hosts. (We are the temple he will come to in these end times.)

> Mal 3:2 But who may abide the day of his coming? and who shall stand when he appeareth? for he is like a refiner's fire, and like fullers' soap: (There will be "fiery trials" to go through if we are to be thoroughly cleansed.)

> Mal 3:3 And he shall sit as a refiner and purifier of silver: and he shall purify the sons of Levi, and purge them as gold and silver, that they may offer unto the LORD an offering in righteousness. (Fiery trials will cause the dross in us [our carnal sin nature] to be separated from the gold and silver [that which is like Jesus].)

These next few verses in Revelation 6 will show us what happens inwardly when we go through experiences that are to purify us and purge us as gold and silver. The cleansing process begins with a revelation of something sinful in us. By opening the sixth seal, Jesus shows him something about himself he could not know until Jesus exposed it. The number six reveals the nature of this revelation:

> Six is either 4 *plus* 2, i.e., man's world (4) with man's enmity to God (2) brought in: or it is 5 *plus* 1, the grace of God made of none effect by man's addition to it, or perversion, or corruption of it: or it is 7 *minus* 1, i.e., man's coming short of

spiritual perfection. In any case, therefore, it has to do with *man*; it is the number of imperfection; the human number; the number of MAN as destitute of God, without God, without Christ. (Bullinger)

He has a revelation of his sin and immediately there is an earthquake. Earthquakes have happened at significant events throughout Scripture including at the giving of the law at Mt. Sinai, the death of Jesus, the resurrection of Jesus and the releasing of Paul and Silas from prison. Similarly, as this person in revelation sees and acknowledges his own sin (Mt. Sinai), and dies to it (in Christ), he is resurrected (in Christ) and comes out of his self-imposed prison (Paul and Silas released) and will minister in great power (the jailor and his household saved).

Soon after the revelation of his own sin, there is a great shaking. This is representative of a great trial that we encounter that is necessary to shake out of us all that is in opposition to Christ and bring us into total dependence on him for our physical, spiritual and emotional well being. We can learn a little about the nature of this trial in the last half of this verse: "the sun became as black as sackcloth of hair, and the moon became as blood.

The Sun and the Moon

I can think of a few scenarios that could cause the sun to appear black. One would be from the eruption of several volcanoes worldwide. However, our interpretation here is inward; therefore, our interpretation must be spiritual in nature. Just as life in our solar system is dependent upon our sun, even so our lives are dependent upon Jesus Christ, God's Son, and our relationship with him. If the Son is black to us, it must mean that we have lost our ability to experience God's presence. It is not that he would leave us, but our perception will be that he has done so. It is then that all we can do is walk by faith. The moon is a biblical type of our faith. Blood represents our life (Lev 17:11). When we have lost the sense of God's presence, all we can do is live by faith.

Verse and Interpretation

Rev 6:12 And I beheld when he had opened the sixth seal, and, lo, there was a great earthquake; and the sun became black as sackcloth of hair, and the moon became as blood;

When Jesus revealed to me my sin showing how far short I was from the standard of perfection in Jesus Christ (opening the sixth seal), I went through a great trial (a great earthquake). I totally lost all perception of the presence of Jesus in my life (sun became black as sackcloth of hair). All I could do was hold onto faith (moon) for my very life (blood).

* * * * * * * * * * * * * * * * * * *

Rev 6:13 And the stars of heaven fell unto the earth, even as a fig tree casteth her untimely figs, when she is shaken of a mighty wind.

Here are some of the things that happen when we go through this great trial that occurs with the opening of the sixth seal. When we have been enjoying the presence of God and suddenly we can't seem to perceive him at all, we begin to search everywhere in our attempts to determine what God wants to accomplish in us through this trial. It is not that he wants us to suffer, of course, but it is only in these difficult times that we stretch ourselves to the limit of our endurance in seeking God. In this time of great longing we are willing to examine everything we believe and understand in order to determine where we have missed God. This is when the stars of heaven begin to fall.

Stars

In Scripture, stars can represent people. God told Abram his seed would be as numerous as the stars of the heavens. In Joseph's dream the sun, moon and eleven stars bowed down to him. So we have strong scriptural precedents for saying these stars represent people. Since these stars here in Rev 6:13 are in the heavens, these must be people who have high positions in the church.

When we are going through trials and seeking answers to help us through our difficulty, we often turn to the teachings of other Christians, especially those who are well-known and have large followings. There is something about the nature of trials, the ones that are intended to bring us into greater maturity, that open our eyes to the shallowness of many church teachings. At this stage in our spiritual development, we have diligently searched the scriptures for ourselves and learned that some of the things being taught in the churches are shallow or immature in interpretation. In fact we may even have found them to be heretical. In this way, people that we held in high esteem fall in our eyes. We can no longer sit under their teaching. Their books are no longer of interest to us. In fact, the whole idea of church hierarchy falls. The more we mature in Christ, the more we see how the present church structure has diminished the beautiful truth of the priesthood of all believers. We begin to see gifts in others that have been smothered under the covering of church hierarchical leadership. So we see here a great shift taking place in this person's whole perception of the church and church leadership. These are the stars that fall from heaven.

Untimely Figs and Wind

As I stated above, the more we mature in Christ the more we see how immature some of the concepts we once believed actually are. Our English word "immature" is from the Latin *immaturus* which means "untimely, unripe." These old understandings are untimely and unripe like the figs here in Revelation that fall off the tree when a mighty wind blows. The mighty wind that is blowing here reminds me of what the apostles heard at Pentecost. "And suddenly there came a sound from heaven as of a rushing mighty wind, and it filled all the house where they were sitting."

When we go through trials and we seek God with all our heart, mind, soul and strength, old immature beliefs and ways of doing things will fall away like unripe figs off a tree due to the great infilling of the Holy Spirit who comes to all who truly seek him.

I sense a great trial shortly coming upon the church in the Western world. This trial will cause all Christians to seek God as they have never sought him before. The trial I speak of is jihad. Untold millions of militant Muslims have gone out all over the world as 'refugees." They call them "rape-fugees" in Germany. Our US government has been secretly bringing into this country millions of Muslims over a period of several years. Many years ago a friend of mine sat next to a woman on an airliner whose job it was to assist Muslims in resettlement to the US. This was before the tremendous influx of Muslims out of Syria and the Middle East en mass in 2015-16. Jihad against Christians has been going on in Middle Eastern countries for several years (but mostly unreported in our mainstream news), but we have never thought it could happen in America. We are going to see that we have been wrong.

As more and more Americans realize their freedoms have been signed away by the stroke of the presidential pen and their prosperity stolen by the powers that be in government and banking, there will be tremendous anguish and paralyzing fear. Out of this loss many will begin to seek God fervently. Organized Christianity will disband because it will no longer be safe to meet openly in church buildings. The true church will go underground. Multitudes will die just as they did in Hitler's Germany only it will be worse.

If all this seems unbelievable we have to remember that this is the harvest, the end of the world as we have known it. During the harvest we will see the fullness of evil and the fullness of good at the same time. As the fullness of evil manifests in its attempts to destroy the earth and the people on it, the fullness of God is going to manifest in his body on earth. Many will come to perfection. Lest we get discouraged, Peter reassures us there will be a new heaven and a new earth.

Verse and Interpretation

Rev 6:13 And the stars of heaven fell unto the earth, even as a fig tree casteth her untimely figs, when she is shaken of a mighty wind.

Church leaders and doctrines I had trusted fell in my eyes (the stars of heaven fell unto the earth) as they now seemed to be immature and no longer applicable to what I was learning to be true about God and his church (as a fig tree casteth her untimely figs). This was because of the great infilling of the Holy Spirit I was experiencing (when she is shaken of a mighty wind).

* * * * * * * * * * * * * * * * *

Chapter Twelve

The Transformation of Our DNA

Rev 6:14 And the heaven departed as a scroll when it is rolled together; and every mountain and island were moved out of their places.

In the previous verse this person is moving forward with God in a powerful way. He has been willing to set aside his immature and incomplete beliefs about God and the church. The Holy Spirit has come to him in a powerful way. The words "mighty wind" are suggestive of the great infilling of the Holy Spirit received by the one hundred twenty believers in the upper room in Acts. This is a major infilling of the Holy Spirit. Our willingness to cast aside our old understandings is vital in order for God to fill us with his Spirit in the powerful way he wants for us in these end times. These are cataclysmic times on earth and we will only overcome by means of a radical departure from the old traditions and an embracing of all the new end time revelations God has for us. This is difficult for many believers because of their fears of believing something New Age or heretical, but just because something seems new it is not necessarily non-biblical. The fact is there are things the church has believed for centuries that are not truly biblical—such as forsaking the priesthood of all believers for the hierarchical hegemony seen in our churches today.

We need to reexamine what Paul taught in 1 Corinthians 13:

> Charity (love) never faileth: but whether there be prophecies, they shall fail; whether there be tongues, they shall cease; whether there be knowledge, it shall vanish away. For we know in part, and we prophesy in part. But when that which is perfect is come, then that which is in part shall be done away. When I was a child, I spake as a child, I understood as a child, I thought as a child: but when I became a man, I put away childish things. For now we see through a glass, darkly; but then face to face: now I know in part; but then shall I know even as also I am known (1 Cor 13:8-12). (Parentheses mine.)

Our key to not being deceived, I believe, is love—love for God and love for the brethren. This must be a pure love not based on any selfish ends but a sacrificial love that is willing to lay down one's life for another. Additionally we need to be in relationship with other believers with whom we pray, worship and study. Any particular truth will be seen many places in the Bible, not in just one verse. It is also important for it to be seen in context.

Some people insist there is no new revelation for the church of the end times. I say there has to be because never in the 2000 year history of the church has there been a time when the whole earth was destructing—rapidly! If people knew what is actually happening to our one and only beautiful earth, they would go into panic mode. Christians without strong faith would also panic. What is happening today is absolutely unbelievable. Our world leaders are insanely following demon spirits, many of which are disguised as aliens from other planets. They are working at eradicating the lives of billions of people with the goal of permitting only 500 million to live. All this is to be accomplished by mandates such as Agenda 21 from the United Nations. Meanwhile they are polluting the entire earth with radiation, destroying the ozone layer, killing off the plants God created for us to have for food and for medicine (GMO and glyphosate), destroying the oceans, and a whole list of other things including polluting the human gene pool.

Yet in the midst of all this, there will be people coming into the fullness of Christ with bodies that cannot be destroyed by any of these things. There will also be a tremendous number of deaths even amongst Christians. But for those who sincerely love and seek God, there will be the awesome experience of his coming personally to each one as a bridegroom to his bride. After this initial coming where the spiritual body is awakened to feel God's touch, the final stages of bringing us to completion in spirit, soul and body will commence.

Now that I've laid the groundwork for my interpretation of Rev 6:14, let's see what happens to this believer after the mighty rushing wind of the Holy Spirit comes upon him and he sees that many things he used to believe make no sense at all in light of his new experience with God. This is all done in a process that takes place over time but a relatively short period of time.

The Heaven Departed

What is the heaven spoken of here? It is defined in Strong's as "air, the sky and the abode of God." According to some of the early Church Fathers, allegorically it represents the understanding opened. Before continuing our interpretation of heaven, we need to see exactly what it did in this verse. It departed as a scroll. The Greek word used here for departed is *apochorizo*, which can also mean to separate; "to rend apart; reflex. to separate" (Strong's). *Apochorizo* appears only one other time and that is in Acts 15:39 where Paul and Barnabas parted company over the issue of Mark:

> And the contention was so sharp between them, that they departed asunder (*apochorizo*) one from the other:

Based on this rendering of *apochorizo* we could accurately say that the heavens separated. For our inward spiritual interpretation we are not speaking about the sky overhead but about the abode of God where angels dwell. We sometimes speak of having an open heaven. This means that the veil that separates us from the spiritual realm is pulled back such that we can view something in that dimension that has been closed to us. In our imperfect human state, we are not permitted to see into heaven except for a brief vision or dream whereby God allows us to view something. As we mature into the fullness of Christ in the end times, the Lord is going to separate that veil for us so we can see into that realm. This will be necessary for our survival as the NWO applies all the weapons in its demonic arsenal to destroy humanity and the earth. We will have the angels of heaven guiding us and helping to provide food and all manner of life's necessities as those ruling the world make and brutally enforce their laws designed to kill us. Just by way of example, while the NWO sprays our skies with coal sludge, heavy metals and chemicals so we can't even see the sun, they pass laws blaming "we the people" for destroying the atmosphere! In Canada now everyone who heats their home with wood, must register their wood burning stoves. They are to get rid of these stoves within three years and buy something that very likely most people can't afford that supposedly won't pollute the environment. In the US they are also cracking down on stove manufacturers and distributors. People who believe the lie about climate change will probably comply. The mainstream media keeps the masses unaware of what is happening before their very eyes!

We see a prophetic glimpse of an open heaven in John 1 where Nathanael approaches Jesus and Jesus says, "Behold, an Israelite indeed in whom there is no guile." Soon after that he says, "Verily, verily, I say unto you, hereafter ye shall see heaven open, and the angels of God ascending and descending upon the Son of man." First of all, Jesus commented on Nathanael's character. To have no guile is to have no deceit, to be pure in heart. Then he said he would see heavenly things. We must be pure in heart in order to have an open heaven because we see according to what is in our heart. God is working in our lives, allowing trials and challenges in order to give us an opportunity to make godly decisions so he can work in us to transform our life into the very likeness of Jesus.

As a Scroll When It Is Rolled Together

I must ask the question, how is it that the heavens are opened to us? What takes place that makes this possible? I believe the answer lies in the words "as a scroll is rolled together." This is how the heavens are opened—as a scroll is rolled together. What is a scroll? It is something on which a message is written. This message is rolled together. Strong's tells us that rolled together, *heilisso*, is a form of the verb, *heilo*, which means "to coil or wrap."

So here we have a message that is rolled together or coiled. This has to be the DNA molecule! Our DNA has messages on it. It is in a coil form consisting of the double helix. If you have ever seen a picture of it in a cell you've seen that the DNA is actually quite long and is coiled back and forth upon itself within the cell. In this ancient book written two thousand years ago is a passage about the DNA molecule, something that was not even discovered until the late 19th century! (Most people think the DNA molecule was discovered in the mid 20th century, but it was actually first seen by a Swiss chemist named Friedrich Miescher. It was not widely accepted by scientists until the work of Watson and Crick in the mid 1900s.)

Our interpretation for "And the heaven departed as a scroll when it is rolled together" is:

and the heavenly realm where God and his holy angels dwell was opening to me according to what was encoded in my DNA.

I find this totally amazing in light of what I have been learning and experiencing in the past few weeks. By a series of circumstances that I know the Lord arranged, a book came into my possession entitled, *Feelings Buried Alive Never Die* by Karol K. Truman. In this book she explains how feelings buried in our subconscious mind determine how we make decisions and live our lives. We can identify these feelings and transform them at the very level of our DNA. Every physical pain and sickness can be traced back to feelings hidden in our subconscious mind that need to be changed. In this book is something she calls "The Script." It is a way of, according to her, asking our own spirit to go to the subconscious mind and change and heal our feelings at their origin recorded in our DNA.

This book seems a little "New Age" to me and therefore at another time and circumstance I might not have read it, but this was the right time and circumstance. I have found in this book powerful truths I recognize as absolutely Christian in nature. For me as a Christian I choose to use the Script as a prayer and I ask Jesus to do the things she says our spirit can do. I know my spirit is united with God's spirit so either way the Lord is doing it. All these negative things in our subconscious mind are encoded in our DNA. I know my DNA is changing as I pray. I know this because my body is being healed of things I have struggled with my entire life. Little did I know there was sinful thinking and feeling lodged in my subconscious mind at the level of my DNA that caused my disease. As I've been reading more about DNA I am learning that we actually put messages into our DNA according to what we experience and choose in life.

I have always enjoyed excellent health but eczema was something that could make me miserable. However, with prescription creams I managed quite well until a few months ago when I called the pharmacy to have my prescription refilled. Just as I was about to finish my order, the Lord said, "No."

My first thought was that he must be going to heal me. However, nothing happened and eczema started to rage like never before. I had to get up at night, sometimes more than once, and apply my peppermint essential oil to stop the itching. In *Feelings Buried Alive Never Die* under the heading of possible feelings in the subconscious mind related to eczema, the author listed the following: "over sensitive, feeling you are being interfered with or prevented from doing something and therefore frustrated, unresolved hurt feelings and unresolved feelings of irritation." Although I was not aware of these things in my life now, I certainly identified with them being in my past—or so I thought it was all in the past but it was still buried in my subconscious mind and apparently erupting as disease in my physical body.

As I have prayed according to the Script the eczema seems to be lessening. I have found that the longer a condition has been in your body, the longer it will take to get it out. I cannot remember a time in my life when I did not have eczema. My approach to this healing is multifaceted however. The Script, along with praying and visualizing the healing scriptures, strict obedience to Jesus, changes in diet and removal of chemical-laden soaps, lotions, etc. have all been part of my healing process.

I have learned that often physical problems may be just calling our attention to lies or sin lodged in our subconscious mind. When the lie or sin is removed, the physical affliction will improve or sometimes even be healed. Also God will permit something to get worse so we'll do something about it. I was not bothered by eczema as long as I had my creams. Had I continued in that state I might not have been motivated to do the necessary spiritual work. Without medicine I was totally miserable. The cream that I was not allowed to refill was the one that kept my skin from breaking out. I still had the steroid cream that healed the eruptions and also the moisturizing creams. However, the steroid just couldn't handle the eruptions that flared up after the one medication was withheld.

It is my desire to be free of all pharmaceutical medications. I believe this would be a good goal for all God's people. By doing our spiritual work now, if the medicine is not available in the future, we will have paved the way for a natural healing or possibly even a supernatural healing. All it takes is an economic disaster or breakdown in society and medicine may not be accessible or affordable.

ObamaCare has caused health insurance costs to skyrocket. Some doctors are choosing to leave their practices because of the hassle of government red tape and other problems associated with it. In fact, I had an experience last week that may be an unwelcome prophecy of things to come. I went to my doctor to get a prescription for the steroid cream I am still allowed to use. When I went to the pharmacy to get it, I was told it was no longer on my insurance. It would now cost me $300 for one tube. Thankfully for me, it was still covered by my insurance in another form either as a lotion or an ointment.

Let's look at my interpretation once more:

And the heaven departed as a scroll when it is rolled together is interpreted as "and the heavenly realm where God and his holy angels dwell (heaven) was opening to me (departed) based on the negative messages in my DNA being transformed into the perfection God always intended to be in my DNA (rolled together)."

What will it be like for this heavenly realm to be opened to us? I believe we will see angels, departed saints and even Jesus. The demons of hell, who can only operate in secrecy, will have no place to hide because we will see them, spoil their plans and strip them of their power. We will be able to see what is in people's hearts in order to help them come to repentance and maturity in Jesus Christ.

I think we will see more than just an occasional brief glance via a vision or dream. I believe that once we are changed at the very DNA level of our being, we will be perfected such that we can actually experience being a citizen of that realm. This will require being perfect in spirit, soul and body. We have tended in the Western world to separate these three elements of our being, but they are very much interconnected. As we are seeing here, what we believe in our mind determines to a certain extent what is encoded in our DNA that affects our body.

I believe being in heaven while on earth includes having a perfect body. In order to have a perfect body, we must have a perfect heart. Only the pure in heart can see God; therefore, if we are to see into the realm where he dwells, we must be pure in heart. "Beloved, now are we the sons of God, and it doth not yet appear what we shall be: but we know that, when he shall appear, we shall be like him; for we shall see him as he is. And every man that hath this hope in him purifieth himself, even as he is pure" (1 John 3:2, 3).

Of course there are certain conditions in our bodies that cannot be changed by purifying our heart such as amputated limbs, missing teeth, irreversible paralysis and such like, but if we do all we can to be pure in heart, I am certain we will see God perform miracles of a magnitude we have never seen. Our God is able to regenerate missing body parts or anything else needful for us to have a perfect body.

Mountains

Now we continue on with this verse to see what happens as the heavens are opened and we are changed at the level of our DNA…"and every mountain and island were moved out of their places." For my spiritual interpretation of mountains I turn to the words of John the Baptist:

> Prepare ye the way of the Lord, make his paths straight. Every valley shall be filled, and every mountain and hill shall be brought low; and the crooked shall be made straight, and the rough ways shall be made smooth (Luke 3:4b, 5).

Obviously John was not speaking of literal topography here but of a spiritual preparation that was to make people more receptive to Jesus and his message. As we prepare for Jesus' second coming we are to do the same thing and that is to remove out of our lives anything that would hinder our ability to receive Jesus. We are preparing the way for him to come in us and then we will help others understand how he wants to come in them as well. Jesus is coming to his bride. This is personal and intimate. We will experience him in a way that makes us feel we are the only one and we have his full attention and deepest love at all times. This is so much better than looking up in the clouds along with millions of people and seeing him up there distant and remote. People who do not have the personal experience of Jesus coming within will see him in his Body. They will see the fullness of Christ in his people all over the world.

Mountains are obstructions. If we want to see into the

heavens and experience that glorious realm, the mountains have to be "brought low." Strong's definition for mountain states, "a mountain, (as lifting itself above the plain)." For my interpretation, mountains represent pride because when we lift ourselves up above others, we are prideful. Andrew Murray says that pride is the root of every sin and evil. He continues by saying:

> Jesus Christ took the place and fulfilled the destiny of man, as a creature, by His life of perfect humility. His humility is our salvation. And so the life of the saved ones, of the saints, must needs bear this stamp of deliverance from sin, and full restoration to their original state; their whole relation to God and man marked by an all-pervading humility. Without this there can be no true abiding in God's presence, or experience of His favor and the power of His Spirit; without this no abiding faith, or love or joy or strength. Humility is the only soil in which the graces root; the lack of humility is the sufficient explanation of every defect and failure. Humility is not so much a grace or virtue along with others; it is the root of all, because it alone takes the right attitude before God, and allows Him as God to do all.

So long as we have pride within, we will not be able to see into or experience the heavenly realm. We must be like Jesus to enter there. It is quite clear now that every mountain (pride) has to be moved out of its place if we are to progress into perfection. This dealing with pride that moves the mountain out of its place is a process wherein as we cooperate with God and obey his instructions, he works in us to destroy the pride. Without his help we cannot see how deeply ingrained in us it is.

Islands

An island is something that is separated from the mainland. It is isolated and alone. If one is to go there, one needs to build a bridge, or go in a boat or airplane. We have an area in Upstate New York called the Thousand Islands. Some of these multiple islands, many only large enough for one house, are inhabited by rich people and organizations such as The Skull and Bones Society—people and organizations that obviously want to be left alone. These islands in the Saint Lawrence Seaway remind me of the way many of us are inside. As Dietrich Bonhoeffer said in his book *Ethics* regarding the spiritual condition of humankind:

> Man's life is now disunion with God, with men, with things, and with himself.

When we feel criticized, hurt, disappointed or rejected we have a tendency to withdraw from others and even from our true self within. If we had our own island somewhere we would probably go there—but most of us don't so we just separate within. When we come into the fullness of Christ we must become whole within; therefore, our internal separations (islands) need to be removed.

Verse and Interpretation

Rev 6:14 And the heaven departed as a scroll when it is rolled together; and every mountain and island were moved gout of their places.

And the heavenly realm where God and his holy angels dwell (heaven) was opening to me based on the negative messages in my DNA being transformed into the perfection God always intended to be in my DNA (as a scroll when it is rolled together). And pride (every mountain) was being removed from my life along with the fragmentation (island) caused by all the times I separated from myself, God and others.

* * * * * * * * * * * * * * * * *

Rev 6:15, 16 And the kings of the earth, and the great men, and the rich men, and the chief captains, and the mighty men, and every bondman, and every free man, hid themselves in the dens and in the rocks of the mountains; And said to the mountains and rocks, Fall on us, and hide us from the face of him that sitteth on the throne, and from the wrath of the Lamb:

In this outward account of an inward reality the people mentioned are mostly influential people—kings, great men, rich men, chief captains, and mighty men. Five categories of powerful and influential people are named here followed by two that represent more common men. This is most important for our inward interpretation where a person is being perfected at the level of his DNA. Just as these leaders and great men of the earth control the activities of men, our DNA controls the activities of the cells of our body.

There are even bondmen and free men in our DNA. The following describes the purpose of bonds (bondmen) in the DNA structure:

> A number of factors are responsible for the stability of the DNA double helix structure, among them hydrogen bonds. Internal and external hydrogen bonds stabilize the DNA molecule. The two strands of DNA stay together by H bonds that occur between complementary nucleotide base pairs. Two

hydrogen bonds occur between the adenosine and the thymine base pairs, and between the cytosine and the guanine there are three. (Rafael)

A free man is not in bonds. He is free to go places. For my interpretation he is described below as the RNA that breaks away from the DNA to travel around the cell as a messenger:

> The sequence of bases in a DNA molecule serves as a code by which genetic information is stored. Using this code, the DNA synthesizes one strand of ribonucleic acid (RNA), a substance that is so similar structurally to DNA that it is also formed by template replication of DNA. RNA serves as a messenger for carrying the genetic code to those places in the cell where proteins are manufactured. (Bonner)

Hiding

What does it mean for our DNA to hide from God in the dens and rocks of the mountains? Only something evil would want to hide from God. The good would be irresistibly drawn to him and desire him. Hide from God was the first thing Adam and Eve did when they sinned in the Garden. That was the beginning of sin, death and all the suffering that has plagued all living things since that time. Something was embedded in our DNA all those thousands of years ago that causes us to have a tendency to disobey God, hide from him, do selfish evil things, succumb to sickness, grow old and die.

All this evil we inherited in our genes from our ancestors wants to hide from God in the dens and the rocks of mountains—our own spiritual darkness and pride—but, thankfully, nothing can hide anywhere from our Almighty,

Omnipresent God. What appears destructive from the outward perspective of this verse is actually a great blessing for our inward interpretation because God will destroy all in our DNA that causes sickness, weakness and death.

Hiding - Outward View

As the ensuing verses explain, these people are hiding from God because they are wicked and they fear his wrath. What we see outwardly in our world is just a mirror image of what is in humankind's heart and in our DNA. Almost all world rulers today are evil. They do charitable deeds and claim they want to protect and care for us, but behind closed doors where the evening news' cameras never roll, there is great evil and even Satan worship. While Christians are anticipating the return of Christ, the Satanists are doing all they can to hasten the coming rule of the Antichrist and a One World Government. This is only possible because the hearts of people are evil—everywhere. We either vote these wicked ones into office or we turn the other way and tolerate the evil so long as it doesn't affect us personally. Well, it does affect us personally whether we know it or not because they are destroying civilization as we have known it and the whole physical earth along with it.

Governments all over the world are literally doing what this scriptural passage says. World leaders and their militaries have made underground living quarters and stocked them with several years' worth of supplies. One of the most famous is under Cheyenne Mountain in Colorado. There are tunnels leading from the Denver airport to the hideout under Cheyenne Mountain. These sanctuaries are called Deep Underground Military Bases or DUMBS. There are even some under the oceans!

Whatever these leaders and their militaries (bondmen) know, they're not telling us. The heaven departing as a scroll when it is rolled together makes me think of a nuclear explosion or several simultaneous nuclear explosions. If these leaders were not evil, they would be making provision for their people or at least warning us so we could build our own shelters—but they're not saying anything. Thanks to alternative news sources online there is a great deal of information on this subject. Many of these news sources are Christians who have friends in high places, whistleblowers, who divulge information to them. However, because of compartmentalization none of them has the whole picture.

However bleak all this may appear, our God is totally mindful of it all and everything will fit perfectly into his plans for humanity. I believe it is Judgment Day and we are witnessing that judgment taking place before our very eyes. There will be great outward destruction in the earth but simultaneously God's faithful believers will be changed such that they will not only survive but also enter back into Paradise. When the world leaders and their militaries enter into their underground cities to survive whatever unsurvivable event is going to occur, God's faithful will be changed in their DNA as they put on immortality. It is a strange phenomenon that these evil people who are so fearful they have built underground cities and bases in order to survive the coming disasters, are the very ones who have created the disasters in the first place. They themselves are carrying out the judgment of God upon the rest of humanity all the while they think they are hiding from God. They will be severely judged by God.

It is like in the Old Testament. God's people, the Hebrews, repeatedly turned to idols and had to be judged by God. God permitted the enemy nations around them to execute the judgment on them but only after he gave them many warnings through his prophets. Time and again they ignored the prophets and continued on in their idolatry incurring terrible destruction from God upon themselves and their children by the hands of enemy nations. Then God judged the enemy nations.

Sadly, the Church on the earth today has mostly succumbed to idolatry even after repeated warnings from God. We will suffer greatly. Only the most faithful, those who have developed a relationship with God and obeyed him, will put on immortality during this time of great judgment and upheaval.

Verse and Interpretation

Rev 6:15, 16 And the kings of the earth, and the great men, and the rich men, and the chief captains, and the mighty men, and every bondman, and every free man, hid themselves in the dens and in the rocks of the mountains; And said to the mountains and rocks, Fall on us, and hide us from the face of him that sitteth on the throne, and from the wrath of the Lamb:

Just as rich and influential people give plans and instructions for others to carry out, even so our DNA gives instructions to control the actions of the cells of our body. The people are evil which is evident because they want to hide from God. There is evil in our DNA that contains the curse of death put upon all living things at the time of the Fall. We know that just as people cannot hide to escape

God's judgment neither can the DNA that contains the curse of death hide from God.

* * * * * * * * * * * * * * * * * * * *

Rev 6:17 For the great day of his wrath is come; and who shall be able to stand?

We are definitely living in the day of God's wrath which may also be called "the Day of the Lord" in the Old Testament. This is why we see nations and governments falling. This is just the beginning of the destructive things we will see because nothing will be able to stand except for those things that are firmly rooted in Jesus Christ. The economies and currencies of the world are not based in Jesus Christ so they will all fall. We can expect to see failure in all aspects of our civilization and our world. There will be destruction of the church as we know it. Sadly, even though there is "a church on every corner" in much of America, that is not an accurate portrayal of where the hearts of those who call themselves Christians really are. My husband and I can say unequivocally after over forty years in pastoral ministry, that for most Christians church is a social club or a place to salve their conscience without having to take up their cross daily and follow Christ. The Lord is not pleased with the vast majority of his church and the judgment that will fall on her will be devastating beyond belief. However, for the truly faithful there will be glory because we will be changed into his image and no weapon formed against us will prosper.

In 1972, shortly after we entered fulltime pastoral ministry in central Indiana, the Lord sent a prophet into our little country church. His name was Wayne. He lived on one of the farms that surrounded the church although he was not a farmer. He worked as a janitor at a post office in one of the larger towns in the area. Wayne loved God with all his heart and was deep into Bible study and end time truth. He had an incredible gift for prophecy which flowed freely in our nightly prayer meetings at the parsonage. People loved to come to those meetings because they knew they would experience real church there—deep Bible study, prayer, Christian fellowship, and personal words from God. It was a glorious time but it didn't last long.

For the brief seven months we were at that little church, the regular church services were typical for our denomination at that time, but the real meat and potatoes of Christianity was taking place at the parsonage. The established, ingrained and long-term leaders of our little country church were not truly Christians and were incensed over the growth of the church and especially over the prayer meetings. So it didn't take long for them to, behind our backs, appeal to the supervisor and make charges against us that resulted in our choosing to leave that denomination. (Many years later that supervisor apologized to us saying he came to understand that those people were just afraid of losing their control over the church and that we did nothing wrong.)

Wayne would only prophesy when the Spirit of God came upon him in a way that he actually felt. You could always tell when he was going to come forth with a word because as he prayed in tongues, his prayer language would change demonstratively.

At the time we received the prophecies, we naively thought they would come to pass shortly…even momentarily, but years passed and it seemed that nothing was happening. Actually a lot was happening but it was not reported in the mainstream news which at the time was our only news source except for a few news letters from more informed sources. Once computers and the Internet became more available we were able to read alternative news and learn what was actually going on behind the scenes.

Here are a couple of prophecies from that time that are presently occurring:

> My people, hear ye the voice of the Lord this night for I say unto thee this is the day that shall rock the earth, when thou shalt see kingdoms tumble; when thou shalt see the great and mighty brought low. For this is the day of the Lord, when the Lord thy God shall humble man. He shall bring down that which man has built up, for this is an abomination in the sight of the Lord. For thy God is righteous; thy God is holy; thy God is almighty. He shall bring forth that which he hath proclaimed saith the Lord.

> I am about to shake this earth, and I will not only shake the earth but I will shake the heavens also. I shall tear down strongholds that have been built up and I will tear down those things which the Devil hath greatly built up, for I am God and there is none other. There is none other beside me, saith the Lord. And I will tear down those things which have destroyed men's lives and torn them apart. I will build up my kingdom in the earth, saith the Lord, and nothing shall destroy it or come against it, for it is an everlasting kingdom, and nothing shall stand against it. Nothing shall prevail against my church for hath not I said that it would be a glorious church without spot or wrinkle; and that I would pour my Spirit upon her and I would bring her forth as a chaste virgin; and that I will show

her forth in the ages to come; and I will show her before all nations and I will show her before all peoples? And she shall greatly glorify my name, for my name shall be established in her. And I will raise her up and I will put her on high, saith the Lord. And thou shalt see a great thing, saith God, when thou shalt behold my church. Yea, for I gave myself for her because I loved her, saith the Lord. And I shall bring her forth unto my bosom, saith God Almighty.

Some may wonder why, in light of these prophecies, I say the church will be severely judged. It is because so few are hot: "So then because thou art lukewarm, and neither cold nor hot, I will spew thee out of my mouth" (Rev 3:16). Sadly this is where most of the church is—lukewarm. The Lord has put many warnings in his Word regarding how few will actually be saved:

> Enter ye in at the strait gate: for wide is the gate, and broad is the way, that leadeth to destruction, and many there be which go in thereat: Because strait is the gate, and narrow is the way, which leadeth unto life, and few there be that find it (Matt 7:13, 14).

The Greek word for narrow, *thlibo*, is also translated as "affliction, suffer tribulation and trouble." Paul taught his disciples saying, "We must through much tribulation enter into the kingdom of God." There is no other way. It is only through difficulties—difficulties that, if we respond rightly will kill us (our sin nature)—that we can be changed into the image of Christ. The true nature of man is corrupt through and through—that nature must die and be replaced with Christ's nature if we would be perfect.

Now in order to answer the scripture's question, Who shall be able to stand in the great day of his wrath? I turn to the book of Joel. There are many similarities between the description of the destruction of the land detailed in Joel and what is happening in our world today—particularly in the United States. As always the destruction, in whatever form it comes, is the result of God's people being unfaithful to him.

Chapter Thirteen

The Great Army in Joel

Joel begins with the question, has there ever been anything as terrible as this in the history of the Israelites? Immediately this reminds me of today because we are facing disasters never before seen by any inhabitant of earth. We would quickly have to agree that there has never been anything like this. Then Joel elaborates on the destruction of their food caused by plagues of many kinds of locusts:

That which the palmerworm hath left hath the locust eaten; and that which the locust hath left hath the cankerworm eaten; and that which the cankerworm hath left hath the caterpillar eaten (Joel 1:4).

Many people today do not understand that this is exactly our situation all over the earth only it is not insects doing the destruction; it is the New World Order led by insane people following the guidance of demons (locusts, Rev 9:3) possibly masquerading as aliens from other planets. Monsanto has genetically changed the DNA of many of our major foods. These crops cross-pollinate with normal crops and infest them with the same corrupted DNA that does not produce seed that can be replanted. The elite have stored seed in giant vaults in various places around the earth so that some day when the rest of us are "all dead," they can reclaim the earth for themselves and plant unpolluted seeds. You could call that the "palmerworm" in type if you like. (These insects are all locusts of some type or form.) So if the food source is not wiped out by the "palmerworm" what is left will be "eaten" by the "locusts."

Even if our seeds weren't being destroyed by Monsanto's GMO experiments forced on the entire human species, much of our food would still be destroyed because of the death of the honeybees needed to pollinate our crops. The heavy use of pesticides required to grow our genetically altered food in nutrient-depleted soil is killing off the honeybees.

Another destructive force ruining our crops is dreadful weather. Many governments, as part of the United Nations plan to save the earth through depopulation, are controlling the weather. Many countries have this capability including the United States, Russia, China and Great Britain. This control is done through the spraying of heavy metal particulates from aircraft continually flying in the skies of every country on earth. These heavy metal particulates along with whatever else they are spraying hang in the ionosphere where they can receive certain electromagnetic low frequency waves directed at them from various HAARP facilities stationed in strategic places all over the globe. (HAARP stands for High-Frequency Active Auroral Research Program.) In this way weather is being controlled all over the world. What could have been used for good such as causing rain in drought stricken areas is being used for evil to destroy people. It has become a weapon and it is being used by the NWO against the people of the world.

Because of geo-engineering the state of California, where most of our fruits and vegetables are grown, is experiencing its worst drought in history. Orchards that were developed over many decades have been destroyed and cut down. Joel 1:7 states:

He hath laid my vine waste, and barked my fig tree: he hath made it clean bare, and cast it away; the branches thereof are made white.

We live in Western New York State where there are many vineyards. It is often called "wine country" and rivals California for the wines it produces. Last year was one of the worst in history for the grape industry because of lack of sun, too much rain and cool temperatures. One could say, "Well, that was just a bad year." Maybe, but in light of everything else going on, it appears to be more than that. We have had three cool, cloudy (caused by chemtrails) wet summers in a row causing severe damage to some of our crops. The cherry trees have not been able to produce for three years now because with all the wetness, the cherries mold. Without sun, nothing can ripen which has also been a problem. Zucchini squash, which is usually so abundant people don't know what to do with it all, failed last summer. Green beans hardly produced at all. It is easy to see how controlling the weather can ruin crops of all kinds. As Henry Kissinger has stated, "If you control the food supply, you control the people," and that is what the NWO is all about—controlling people. The fig trees in Joel were "barked...clean bare, the branches thereof (were) made white" because the insects ate the bark off the trees. The bark is being removed from the trees in

North America too, particularly in the West, because of radiation pollution from Fukushima. Our government says nothing about it, but radiation levels have increased over 1000 percent in parts of the U.S. since the nuclear disaster in Japan. All marine life in the Pacific Ocean is either dead or dying. Here in Western New York, I see many trees losing their branches from the bottom up with the bark peeling off. There are dead trees everywhere. Some of this is because of radiation and some is because of the metal particulates being sprayed. The roots of the trees have become coated with aluminum such that they cannot absorb water. No matter how much it rains the trees look like they have died because of lack of water—and they have.

The disasters in Joel are from the Lord:

Alas for the day! for the day of the LORD is at hand, and as a destruction from the Almighty shall it come (Joel 1:15).

The food supply was devastated including the corn, grapes, barley, olives, wheat, apples, figs, pomegranates, dates, cattle, sheep and all the beasts of the field. Today we are living in the age that is entering into the final judgment of God. The things being done that are destroying the earth are not directly from God because they are coming through human instruments. However, God has permitted it and all things will work together to achieve his purpose for the consummation of time and the entrance of his kingdom onto the earth.

My prophetic friend mentioned in the beginning of this book had a vision a few years ago where she saw Jesus standing on top of the Empire State Building in New York.

He was holding an egg in his hand. He said the egg represented the United States of America, and then he dropped the egg over the edge. He said he has turned his back on this nation because even his church has turned against him. They won't stand up for his Word, or live by the Word and some are even embarrassed to say his name. He said many people who fall in this category will cry out to him when this happens, but he will not answer them. However, he will remain very close to those who have been faithful to him.

We need to take a serious look at the church today. It doesn't look any different than the world. There are just as many divorces, adulteries (pastors in particular), abortions and other sins as seen in those who don't profess to know Christ. Many true believers have left the church to meet in homes. Some aren't going anywhere because they can't find others of like mind. Due to my Skype ministry, I hear of many church experiences of persons in other countries who have found the church to not be a safe place. They have given up on it.

I truly believe the Lord is calling his faithful believers out of the church because of the great judgment about to fall on it. There is great persecution coming against the church of the Western world that will rival Nazi Germany with its concentration camps. Already Christians, even children, are actually being beheaded in some Middle Eastern countries. The government of the United States has done nothing to help those Christians but has opened our borders to the Muslim "refugees" who are now entering our cities and towns, taking American jobs and free government assistance, which will decimate our already troubled economy. Some are demanding that Sharia law take over (which has already happened in Dearborn, Michigan) thereby nullifying our Constitution which has basically been dismantled anyway by some of our most recent Presidents. Truly these are the last of the last days.

As Jesus said, we must look up for our redemption draweth nigh. Many aspects of what this redemption will entail have been disclosed on the pages of this book. This book was written with the intention that when all hell breaks loose in the world and you suddenly feel the gentle presence of Jesus as described in this book, you will know that he has come to you and awakened your spiritual body. You will understand how he will speak to you and guide you in your final preparations to come into perfection and put on immortality.

In the midst of all the darkness and peril seen in Joel 1, God tells of his great army that will be going forth into all the earth:

Blow ye the trumpet in Zion, and sound an alarm in my holy mountain: let all the inhabitants of the land tremble: for the day of the LORD cometh, for it is nigh at hand; A day of darkness and of gloominess, a day of clouds and of thick darkness, as the morning spread upon the mountains: a great people and a strong; there hath not been ever the like, neither shall be any more after it, even to the years of many generations (Joel 2:1, 2).

Here in this verse we see something I have observed elsewhere in Scripture—that at the time the world faces its greatest darkness, God's people will experience the greatest light. The people of God are described in the above scripture as being "...a great people and a strong; there hath not been ever the like, neither shall be any more after it, even to the years of many generations." This is an aspect of the second coming of Christ and the final judgment on the world that is seldom ever taught—that in the midst of the greatest suffering, there is going to be a great ministry going forth through God's people. (There is a teaching that all the Christians will be "raptured" off the earth and some Jewish people will have a great ministry, but that is false teaching. You don't reject Christ as the Jews have done and then suddenly become the people described here in Joel. It takes many years of suffering, struggle and sacrifice to come to this level of maturity and power in Christ.)

As we delve into this passage it would be good to remember that Scripture can be viewed on different levels and with different interpretations and this is in accordance with the plan and purpose of God. His Word is intended to be for all people at all times. Having said that, I would like to point out that any commentary I consulted on Joel 2 (which was very few) said that the people here were locusts. This would be their interpretation based on the context. However, if we approach this passage with the revelation of God for the end times in mind, (something the commentators didn't have), then we can view them as being people which is in accordance with the definition of the Hebrew word for people used in the passage. According to Strong and his numbering system, people is "5971. 'am, am; from H6004; a people (as a congregated unit); spec. a tribe (as those of Israel); hence (collect.) troops or attendants; fig. a flock:--folk, men, nation, people." Therefore, in my opinion, commentators are stretching it a little bit to say that these people are locusts. Let's look further in the Joel passage to see some of the characteristics of these people.

> *Joel 2:3 A fire devoureth before them; and behind them a flame burneth: the land is as the garden of Eden before them, and behind them a desolate wilderness; yea, and nothing shall escape them.*

This is not speaking here of literal fire or literal flame but spiritual realities. Fire is consistently used throughout the Bible in the sense of being something that purifies and cleanses. Flame has to do with passion. (We might refer to a former romantic interest as being an "old flame.")

This verse speaks of two characteristics about these people. The first is they have a ministry of judgment that will purify and cleanse others. If the rest of the church is to come up out of its lethargy and ignorance of spiritual realities, it is going to have to be judged. These people, wherever they go, will be able to tell people what is in their heart that is separating them from God and holding them back from perfection. They will minister in such a way that people will repent and their sins will be burned out of them. They will be purified. This happens as the great army goes forward. The flame that burns behind them is the new passion for God that has been stirred in the hearts of those who received the ministry of judgment from their hands.

Secondly, the land as the Garden of Eden before them speaks of the life of these ministers themselves. They are in the same spiritual realm Adam and Eve were in with one major difference being that these people are mature. Adam and Eve were immature in that they knew nothing about sin and its consequences. These people have known sin and overcome it through the Lord Jesus Christ. They are ready to lead the way for others to go back to the garden. The wilderness behind them reveals the wilderness of suffering and sacrifice they came through to get to this place in Christ.

To say "nothing shall escape them" means that they have great discernment. They will know what is in people's hearts even as Jesus knew. This is because Jesus will be in them ministering. What we see here in this passage is the Body of Christ that has been joined with the Head and now ministers in the fullness of Christ.

The appearance of them is as the appearance of horses; and as horsemen, so shall they run (Joel 2:4.)

They have the appearance of horses. Horses, in this instance, represent biblical truths as can be seen in the following verse from Habbakkuk where it says of the Lord:

> ...thou didst ride upon thine horses and thy chariots of salvation (Hab 3:8).

The Lord does come to us riding on truth in that we can only know about him by hearing the truth. After all he *is* the way, the truth and the life. The chariots pulled by the horses can represent the doctrines that arise because of the truth, such as the doctrine of salvation seen here.

Here in Joel these people have the appearance of truth (horses.) This says to me that they look like truth. In other words, they live the truth. They don't just talk about it. To look at them is to see that they are different and the truth is all through them. They are so filled with the Spirit of Jesus that people can just look at them and see that they embody truth. That is going to be so fantastic because today people are constantly lied to by politicians, advertisers, and media to the point they don't know what is true anymore. "Scientists" and "researchers" come up with all sorts of "truths" to prove that Jesus never did miracles; that Jesus married Mary Magdalene and all other sorts of nonsense. People are confused. But when they see these ministers, they will recognize that they embody the truth. They will know that Jesus in them is the truth and that they can be believed. Then there will be great revival and many will believe.

Like the noise of chariots on the tops of mountains shall they leap, like the noise of a flame of fire that devoureth the stubble, as a strong people set in battle array (Joel 2:5).

The Hebrew word for noise, *qowl*, can also be defined as "a voice," or "to call aloud" or "proclamation." We saw previously that chariots represent doctrines, in this verse we can easily see that the noise of chariots can also mean "to proclaim doctrines." This represents preaching the gospel or teaching the Word of God. So that is what these people are doing. They are proclaiming the Word of the Lord.

Many good things take place on mountains in regard to the revelation and activity of God to and for his people:

Micah 4:1 But in the last days it shall come to pass, that the mountain of the house of the LORD shall be established in the top of the mountains, and it shall be exalted above the hills; and people shall flow unto it.

This is what these ministers in Joel 2 will be doing as they leap on the tops of mountains. They will be preaching and teaching the Word of the Lord and in so doing they will be establishing the true church in the end times which will be the house of the Lord. Their proclamation of the gospel will be a purifying word of repentance (flame of fire) that will convict people of their sins. As they repent, the stubble of their carnal nature will burn up. It will be as Paul taught:

> Now if any man build upon this foundation gold, silver, precious stones, wood, hay, stubble; Every man's work shall be made manifest: for the day shall declare it, because it shall be revealed by fire; and the fire shall try every man's work of what sort it is. If any man's work abide which he hath built thereupon, he shall receive a reward. If any man's work shall be burned, he shall suffer loss: but he himself shall be saved; yet so as by fire. Know ye not that ye are the temple of God, and that the Spirit of God dwelleth in you? (1 Cor 3:12-16).

This is how the temple of God will be established in the end times. It will not be a building on a mountain in the geographical location known as Jerusalem in Israel. God is far greater than that. His temple will be all over the earth in his people.

Joel 2:6 Before their face the people shall be much pained: all faces shall gather blackness.
The Hebrew word for face, *paniym*, also means presence. Those who are in the presence of these powerful people will be in much pain. This is because they will see Christ in his glory in them (2 Thes 1:10-12). This will immediately convict them of their sin. This is a painful thing, but Jesus

says, "Blessed are they that mourn, for they shall be comforted." We are to mourn when we see our own sin. That is difficult to do these days because we are surrounded by such gross immorality and violence it is hard to recognize our own jealousy, covetousness, ungratefulness, etc. However, there is no way we will be conformed to the image of Christ and join this great army without recognizing our sin, repenting of it and dying to it.

This particular verse in Joel continues by saying, "...all faces shall gather blackness." This Hebrew word interpreted as "gather" also means "grasp." The Hebrew word for blackness has a root meaning "warmth, ruddy glow, illuminated." Seen in context here in Joel 2:6 this means allegorically that the people in the presence of these ministers will grasp something, they will have illumination about something, and that will be their own blackness meaning allegorically their own sin. As they do so with repentance, the sin will be burned up (as seen in the previous verse).

They shall run like mighty men; they shall climb the wall like men of war; and they shall march every one on his ways, and they shall not break their ranks (Joel 2:7).

I find this verse exciting because it is a prophetic description of the church of the end times being in power and unity. Nothing will be able to stop them as they go forward aggressively to tear down that which the enemy has built up—in individuals' lives first and then in the earth itself. This is the church finally going in and claiming the Promised Land (a type of the human soul entering Paradise).

The Hebrew word for mighty men also means giants. This time, no one in this army will be afraid of giants in the land for they will have conquered their own within and thereby have become spiritual giants that the enemy of men's souls will greatly fear. They will go forth to help others conquer their own giants. Then the church will go forth into the world, striking fear into the heart of the enemy and bringing Christ to the multitudes.

Climb the Walls

Most people have unconsciously built up protective walls within to the extent they have lost their true self. They don't know who they are because they have hidden their true self from the pain of life's disappointments and failures (giants). But this mighty ministry will be so high the walls will not stop them. These ministers will see within people and be able to tell them what is hidden behind their walls. They will tell them what they need to do to break them down so they can come out from behind them. The ministers have power to break down walls but each person has to do his own work. It is only as we ourselves stand against the darkness and demons within that we grow and become strong in the Lord.

Order

"Everyone on his ways…" There is order in this great army. No one is intent on doing his own thing or usurping someone else's ministry. Each will minister according to God's directive to him personally. "They will not break ranks…" No one will go off doing his own thing apart from the rest of the body. God designed the church such that we are to function together and in order with each person doing his God-assigned part. That is what we see here.

Joel 2:8 Neither shall one thrust another; they shall walk every one in his path: and when they fall upon the sword, they shall not be wounded.

It has often been said that Christians are the only ones who shoot their own wounded. We have seen that principle at work in the churches we've served over the past forty years. It is amazing how quickly Christians can turn against a fellow Christian who is down and criticize him. This army of the Lord described in Joel will not be like that. "One shall not thrust another" means they will not oppress a fellow Christian. To "walk everyone in his path" means they will tend to their own spiritual walk rather than criticize someone else's unless it is done in humility with the intent of bringing their fellow Christian up to a more spiritual level in the Lord. Jesus taught about this in Matthew and elsewhere. In the following passage, a "mote" actually means a twig.

> And why beholdest thou the mote that is in thy brother's eye, but considerest not the beam that is in thine own eye? Or how wilt thou say to thy brother, Let me pull out the mote out of thine eye; and, behold, a beam is in thine own eye? Thou hypocrite, first cast out the beam out of thine own eye; and then shalt thou see clearly to cast out the mote out of thy brother's eye (Matt 7:3-5).

Sadly this has all too often been what the world has seen of the church, and the world knows a hypocrite when they see one. They may be doing the same themselves, but they realize they are not professing to be something they are not—that is a Christian. John wrote that they will know we are Christians by our love for one another. No wonder the church in the Western world has failed to grow and impact its culture. Too often we Christians act just like people in the world while at the same time claiming we are different because we are Christians.

I must add though that the church has been heavily infiltrated by Satanists. Many a pastor who has fallen because of sexual immorality may not have been a Christian at all. Cults send their young people into the Bible colleges and seminaries to marry the children of authentic Christians to bring them down and also to go into the churches as leaders or teachers in the Bible colleges and seminaries. They may not commit any outwardly visible heinous sin but just the demons they carry can cause strife and division. We must, however, be very careful in our judgments of such situations. Only God can reveal the true intentions of the heart and it takes one close to God with discerning of spirits to identify such ones. God has been teaching us discerning of spirits for several years now, and the things we have discerned we have kept to ourselves only entrusting them to prayer. However this knowledge has been a warning from God to be cautious about whom we trust.

Now to finish this verse… "and when they fall upon the sword, they shall not be wounded." Just looking at this portion it would appear that they cannot be physically harmed, which I do believe. However, I think there is a deeper meaning here that is hidden in the English definitions of the Hebrew words.

- To fall also means to divide.

- Sword can mean the Word. It is not the typical Hebrew word for sword and it can even mean a plant as seen in the following verse: Thy plants are an orchard of pomegranates, with pleasant fruits; camphire, with spikenard, (Song 4:13).
- Wounded also means greedy and gain.

It is important to see here that when these people preach and teach rightly dividing (fall) the Word of truth (sword) they will not be greedy for gain (wounded). We have seen many ministries fall because of their leaders being greedy for gain. I'm sure we have all seen television ministers that preach for ten minutes and sell their wares and ask for money the remaining twenty of the half hour program. I have recently been ministering via Skype to a woman in Germany. She is highly educated and had a high position working for the German government until she became a Christian ten years ago. At that point she came under extreme persecution and suffering such that she could no longer hold a job.

When I first began ministering to her for her abuse issues, I knew she was living on government subsistence but I had no idea she had not eaten for four days which made her extremely weak and even sick. Then I found out she was tithing to a ministry in America! This is how strongly some church people have been taught to give as demonstrated in her having to starve to do so. She was counting on the supernatural of God to provide food for her which didn't happen. Had I known, I would have given her money for food. I am certain the ministry she was giving to in America did not need the money nearly as much as she did!

Chapter Fourteen

An Army Unlimited

Joel 2:9 They shall run to and fro in the city; they shall run upon the wall, they shall climb up upon the houses; they shall enter in at the windows like a thief.

Here we see that those in this army have no limits as to where they can go. For our inward, allegorical view these cities and walls are inside people. Cities can be places where we have stored doctrinal things and walls can be the truths that defend these doctrines. There are a lot of false doctrines in our churches today that these ministers will be able to identify. They will teach end time truths to bring them down. We have only known in part as 1 Corinthians 13 explains, but when that which is perfect comes, these things will be done away with.

This will be a major part of this perfect ministry that God is preparing to bring forth through his Body in these tumultuous times. But first, that which the Devil has built up must come down. That is why our world is in such chaos and upheaval now. Governments and worldly systems are crumbling and beginning to fall. This is all according to God's plan. Even though there is great evil manifesting, it has just been hidden but is now coming out into the open. I know because over the past 24 years that I have ministered for satanic ritual abuse I have realized that the holocaust of WWII never ended; it just went underground. These SRA people have suffered atrocities that are comparable to and beyond what we know went on in the camps. Many of the evil perpetrators who experimented on, tortured and murdered millions of people were brought to the United States in what was called Operation Paper Clip to teach our government to do what they did. These people are all involved in Satanism. They think they are ruling the world and that they will usher in their New World Order and control everyone on the planet, but our Great God has plans far greater, secret plans that will astound the world. As the Word of God plainly teaches, good ultimately defeats evil and the "good guys" win. It is the meek who will inherit the earth.

They shall climb up upon the houses; they shall enter in at the windows like a thief.

Most often we think of a house as representing a person. "Climb" in the Hebrew means to rise up. These great end time ministers will rise up spiritually into a higher realm where they will be able to see inside a person (windows) and know what is hidden in their soul. The Word tells us that Jesus is coming like a thief. His ministers who will be filled with his Spirit are also coming like a thief because Jesus is within them doing the ministry. They will see inside the people and tell them things they need to know in order to progress spiritually. We often don't see our own sin. We don't know what is in our own heart until Jesus reveals it to us. These ministers will be able to do this. They will come into a congregated group of believers, teach the truth that will bring down false doctrines and reveal what is in their hearts that God wants to deal with. This will be a powerful ministry that will be going on worldwide as those who have been prepared in the wilderness of God for this hour, are led forth at the leading of the Holy Spirit to build the great spiritual temple that Jesus will fill with his power and glory.

Joel 2:10 The earth shall quake before them; the heavens shall tremble: the sun and the moon shall be dark, and the stars shall withdraw their shining:

In keeping with this inward interpretation, each noun in this verse will have an allegorical meaning. As we view this in context it appears the earth's quaking and the heavens' trembling will be a result of the ministry coming forth from this great army of the Lord. We will view this verse in three venues: the inward spiritual, the outward spiritual and outward natural.

The Inward Spiritual

The earth represents the natural side of a person with which he understands and interacts intelligently with life on earth. This would include his soul and his physical body. This soul is quaking in the sense that, according to the Hebrew definition of quake, it is experiencing strong emotions and these emotions are felt in the body. I believe he is feeling these emotions because he knows the ministry he is receiving is straight from God. It is not just the words that are spoken that are causing such powerful emotions, but it is the very presence of God that has come upon him during this ministry that is causing such strong emotion.

The heavens represent the spiritual side of this person, and this spiritual side is now trembling. This is specifically speaking of the spiritual body. The spiritual body is now trembling because during the ministry as the Holy Spirit came upon this person, it awakened his spiritual body and he began to feel the gentle undulating motion of an awakened spiritual body as described in my experience in the beginning of this book. The Hebrew word for tremble used here is *ra'ash* and it can mean "to undulate as a field of grain." This gives even more understanding as to why the strong emotions are being felt by the natural side of the person. He has begun to feel the awakening of his spiritual body and he is absolutely stunned and greatly impacted emotionally. It is just an incredible experience to have no knowledge of even having a spiritual body and then to feel it suddenly awaken is astounding. Not only is the awareness of the awakening so amazingly wonderful, but along with this awakening, the person feels God's love. This awakening truly does feel like a deep touch from God—a touch that is like a loving caress repeated over and over again without any end.

The Sun, Moon and Stars

In type the sun represents Jesus who is our light, the moon is the church as a reflection of that light and the stars represent certain ministers or ministries that we have held in high esteem. The powerful impact of this end time ministry that brings the manifest presence of the Holy Spirit with the awakening of the spiritual side will tremendously impact people's former beliefs regarding Jesus, the church and ministries that have been lifted up and most visible. They will realize that their former concept of God (the sun) is dark compared with what they are experiencing now. In fact, this word for dark in the Hebrew can also be interpreted as "foul" or "turbid." When something is turbid it is "not clear or transparent because of stirred up sediment and the like." I believe our view of Jesus has been greatly obscured by the sediment of unbiblical concepts based on the influence of our culture, our experience with our earthly parents, misinterpretation of Scripture, false doctrines in the church many of which are holdovers from the dark ages, along with other factors.

We are going to experience Jesus in such a powerful and yet sweet and gentle way that everything else we've known spiritually will seem dark in comparison. Our whole concept of church will be changed as we see how badly we've "missed it." Ministers and ministries exalted worldwide via the media will come crashing down in our eyes as we realize they were not the lights we thought they were. Any ministry esteemed by governments and media moguls should be highly suspect no matter what we have been told. God's real stars are hidden away laying down their lives so that others might have life.

It is amazing to see how Scripture can be equally true in both inward and outward views. What we have seen here inwardly will be happening outwardly at the same time. Those who have this inward experience will be in absolute ecstasy. At the same time the outward experience will be destroying the world as we have known it along with people who are under God's judgment. Those of us who are moving forward in God will not need to fear because a New Earth (Isa 65:17, Isa 66:22, 2 Pet 3:13, Rev 21:1) is coming. It is the New Jerusalem. It is the Kingdom of God. Even while we are on earth and destruction is all around us, we will be experiencing our long awaited new Kingdom of God. There may be a time of suffering prior to our entry because as the Scripture plainly states, "It is through much tribulation we enter the Kingdom of God." But this suffering is just to destroy that within us that we don't want to take with us anyway—like pride, envy, etc.

An Outward Spiritual View

Many people in the world will quake with fear and trembling when they realize their whole way of life and all they depended on for security and happiness is being destroyed. World leaders have bankrupted their nations through reckless borrowing of money, printing of money and violating all principles of sound financial practices. Soon the prosperity of the Western world will crumble and we will find ourselves in third world living conditions under communism and in some places Sharia law.

The sun and the moon shall be dark and the stars shall withdraw their shining. This can also represent the spiritual condition of the world at this time. People don't know the truth about Jesus (sun) or the truth about his church (moon) that should have been a reflection of him to the earth but was not because of the massive lukewarmness, division and false doctrines in the church. Conditions will be very dark to be sure because of, among other things, the persecution of the church that is coming to the Western world and has already been ongoing in the Muslim countries of the Middle East.

The New World Order leaders have been opening the floodgates for Muslims into previously Christian nations while at the same time promoting communism which is another hater of Christianity. There have been the beheadings of Christians including even children that the mainstream media of the Western world has kept from the unsuspecting populace. Only those who pursue the truth via the many Internet radio and television programs will know what is really happening worldwide.

An Outward Natural View

The earth is definitely quaking. There can be no doubt that we have witnessed a great increase in seismic and volcanic activity occurring worldwide over the last few years. In 2004 a 9.1 earthquake occurred in the Indian Ocean sending a tsunami into Indonesia and other countries in the area resulting in the deaths of over 230,000 people. In 2010 alone we had the great 7.0 quake in Haiti, the 7.7 Sumatran earthquake, and the 8.8 quake in Chili. Each of these resulted in devastating tsunamis that caused tremendous damage and some loss of life. Then in 2011 there was the Japan 9.0 quake and tsunami that decimated parts of Japan and killed many thousands of people.

The heavens are trembling. It is so amazing that evil men are actually fulfilling Scripture in their attempts to control the world. Our atmosphere is trembling because of electromagnetic waves, low frequency electrical waves, scalar waves, WiFi signals, cell phone tower waves and who knows what other kinds of waves that are constantly being projected out into it. There are at least twenty ionospheric heaters around the world projecting various kinds of waves into the ionosphere. Some of these are disrupting the Van Allen Belts which consist of radiation waves that encircle the earth. In short, they are controlling weather, destroying the ozone, heating up the oceans in the wrong places causing massive die-offs of sea creatures and totally destroying the planet.

These ionospheric heaters are called HAARP (High-Altitude Auroral Research Project) and work in conjunction with chemtrails that are daily being sprayed from airplanes all over the world. The spray consists of ashes obtained from coal-burning power plants combined with various heavy metal particulates and strange spiderweb-like microscopic fibers that we all breathe. The spray adversely affects the health of all living things. Just look around you at all the dead and dying trees for example. Day after day the spray blocks our view of the sun or the moon and the stars. In this way the sun, moon and stars are being darkened exactly as this verse in Joel states.

Now here is an amazing fulfillment of biblical prophecy hidden in my interpretation of Joel: The Hebrew word for dark used in this passage is *qadar* and it literally means "to be ashy." Surely the Holy Spirit knew thousands of years ago that men would be spraying a substance made of ashes in the sky that would block the sun, the moon and the stars from our view! This phenomenon would happen around the time that this great army is designated to go forth. I find this astounding. Yes, it is true that pollution in large cities can block our view of the sun, but the chemtrail spraying is going on all over the world.

If you are unfamiliar with the term "chemtrails" do an Internet search on them; you will undoubtedly run across sites that claim they are a conspiracy theory. Dig deeper and you will find multitudinous sites that have indisputable scientific proof of their existence along with many photographs. Look up in the sky whenever you go outside and you will see them there. It is a rare day when they are not spraying. These are differentiated from the normal contrails we've seen behind jet aircraft for many years. A true contrail is thin, short and dissipates in a few minutes. They only appear at high altitudes. Chemtrails are thick and remain all across the sky. They are often spaced at regular intervals so that as the spray spreads in the atmosphere, the chemtrails meet and form a "cloud" cover that eventually obscures the sun from our view. These are sprayed at lower altitudes than where legitimate contrails briefly appear.

Joel 2:11 And the LORD shall utter his voice before his army: for his camp is very great: for he is strong that executeth his word: for the day of the LORD is great and very terrible; and who can abide it?

In order to understand this verse more accurately we need to look at an unimportant-looking word—"before." This word *paniym* in the Hebrew can be translated many different ways, and one of these is "through." I believe the Lord is uttering his voice through his great army. As they go forth to minister, the words they speak are the very words of God. This is why his army is so great.

To "execute" his word is to do his word. This makes us strong. When the word of the Lord is spoken through his great army to his people, if they will do what the Lord has said to do through his ministers, then they will be strong.

This word translated "strong" also means "mighty."

Truly the day of the Lord is great and very terrible. So great and terrible the Scripture asks the question, "Who can abide it." In other words, Who will be able to survive in this terrible time of destruction and turmoil? The answer is the person who does the will of God. The secret to living through all of this is to hear God and obey him. That is all we have to do. We don't have to understand it all or have a pre-thought-out plan. We must just hear and obey. If we have trouble hearing, this mighty ministry will be speaking God's words to us.

So far as working this out in our life, we don't always hear a directive from God other than what is in his Word. If we do righteousness, we are obeying the Word of the Lord. If we love our neighbor as our self, we are hearing the Lord and obeying. However, in the midst of doing this there will undoubtedly be specific *rhema* words because as we consistently obey the commands of Scripture we begin to develop the spiritual faculty of knowing God's ways and God's voice.

Over many years of serving God in the churches, we learned to trust God and follow him. There was never enough money to save for retirement or buy a house, but the Lord consistently said that we were to just follow him day by day and do as he directed. So while friends and family members around us prepared for retirement and bought retirement homes, we lived in a parsonage developing no equity, with just enough money to take care of our needs. But there came a day when God moved mightily on our behalf. He moved us to the mountains of New York and provided the finances for us to buy a little cabin there on seven and a half acres of land. If we had had the resources to go where we wanted and do as we pleased, we would not be in the good position we are in today.

It is a fact that the Lord actually chose our house for us. One morning in June of 2004, we were camping at a campground in the mountains of New York. In my morning prayer, I heard the Lord say, "I have a little house for you." I told my husband who then noticed corroborative scriptures during his devotional time that confirmed what I was hearing.

So after breakfast we headed out to the nearest town to find a real estate agent. We told her what we wanted in a house and what we thought we could afford. She was busy that day but gave us a list of about seven houses that might fit that description and suggested we just drive by them. It was a beautiful early summer's day and we thoroughly enjoyed the prospects of just looking around.

The first house we saw was not what we wanted as it was too close to the road. The second house was so far off the road you could only see it by driving a ways down the driveway which we did. As soon as we saw the little house and the tremendous view of the valley and mountains in front of it, we both immediately know that was the house. We told the realtor who arranged for us to see it inside the next day. We were even more certain after we saw it inside.

It was a Monday morning that the Lord told us about the house and we saw it outside. We saw it inside the next day. We made our offer of considerably less money than the asking price on Wednesday. The owner was out of town on Wednesday and Thursday, but accepted our offer on Friday. It was totally amazing to go from not even thinking about a house to buying one in just five days! We continued living in the church parsonage for another six years and just visiting our new home for two days a week, until the time came for us to leave our denomination and move full time into the cabin. We did not know at the time we bought it that it would become our fulltime home. We just knew it was a good investment for the money we had inherited and that it was God's plan for us.

In closing I would like to sum up some of the things that I believe are most important regarding the message for the end-time church revealed in Revelation 4, 5, 6 and Joel 2.

In the midst of the greatest evil of all time, God's faithful people will experience the fullness of the greatest good of all time. The greatest good was accomplished 2000 years ago when God became a man, dwelt among humanity, died for our sins and rose from the dead. Now we will see the fulfillment of that in and through his body on earth as the people of God fully realize all that God has done for us. The events of the end times and Christ coming to dwell in his body will be far different from what most people have been able to deduce from their Bible studies because of the fact that we have only known in part. With the coming of the Lord's presence to us individually we will have the awakening necessary for us to begin to see the Scriptures in a new light. That which was only in part will pass away because that which is perfect (the Lord Jesus) will have come to us individually and corporately to bring us into the truths and experiences reserved for the church of the end times. God's guidance will be so specific that we will recognize and be able to set aside old inaccurate beliefs and embrace the new as God reveals it to us. Minor sins that we didn't even recognize as sin will be pointed out by him so we can rid our lives of these things. He will perfect his bride.

No matter how dark, polluted, and evil the world becomes, we will have God's supernatural protection and provision for all things. The heavens will be opened to us and we will be able to experience not only God's presence but also the ministry of angels. Even our bodies will be changed such that we will not be harmed by nuclear radiation, poisoned food, air and water or any other destructive force. We will be on earth but also in heaven at the same time. We will minister to others to help them rise up into this glorious place in Christ.

> If ye then be risen with Christ, seek those things which are above, where Christ sitteth on the right hand of God. Set your affection on things above, not on things on the earth. For ye are dead, and your life is hid with Christ in God. When Christ, who is our life, shall appear, then shall ye also appear with him in glory (Col 3:1-4).

What glorious things the church will soon experience in Christ! It will be worth every trial we have had to face in order to enter into his Kingdom. I pray this book will encourage you and help you understand what God is doing in your life as you begin to enter into the final phase of perfection and the fullness of Christ in your life.

Appendix

Verses and Interpretations
Revelation Four

Rev 4:1 *After this I looked, and, behold, a door was opened in heaven: and the first voice which I heard was as it were of a trumpet talking with me; which said, Come up hither, and I will show thee things which must be hereafter.*

After having had many experiences in the church that had developed maturity in my life (after this), I had a totally new experience opened to me that was not of this earth (door opened in heaven). All over my body I began to feel a gentle, slow vibration that was so deep within I knew it was the awakening of my spiritual body (voice of a trumpet). I knew of a certainty that I had received a direct communication from God (voice of a trumpet) in that Jesus had come to me and opened to me a realm in God that had been reserved for his church of the end times (come up hither and I will show thee things which must be hereafter).

Rev 4:2 *And immediately I was in the spirit; and, behold, a throne was set in heaven, and one sat on the throne.*

Immediately I had been lifted up into a spiritual realm (I was in the spirit). My spiritual body (throne) was in a heavenly dimension even though my natural body was still on earth. I knew that Jesus had come to rest upon my spiritual body (one sat on the throne).

Rev 4:3 And he that sat was to look upon like a jasper and a sardine stone: and there was a rainbow round about the throne, in sight like unto an emerald.

I knew that Jesus (he that sat) was making himself known to me through the feeling of his loving presence upon my spiritual body. There was the feeling all over my body of a gentle massage much like one would use when polishing a precious stone (Jasper). The feeling conveyed to me a love deeper than anything I had ever known (sardine stone). This was also the beginning of the preparation of my natural body for putting on immortality (rainbow round about the throne.) New life and vitality were flowing into my natural body (in sight like unto an emerald).

Rev 4:4 And round about the throne were four and twenty seats: and upon the seats I saw four and twenty elders sitting, clothed in white raiment; and they had on their heads crowns of gold.

In the heavenly realm, my spiritual body was under perfect heavenly government (And round about the throne were four and twenty seats). And I understood that my spiritual mind was resting upon my spiritual body (and upon the seats I saw four and twenty elders sitting). My spiritual mind had the qualities of holiness, purity, and overcoming. It had also received the promises of Scripture for those who overcome: incorruptibility, rejoicing, righteousness, life and glory (clothed in white raiment; and they had on their heads crowns of gold).

Rev 4:5 And out of the throne proceeded lightnings and thunderings and voices: and there were seven lamps of fire burning before the throne, which are the seven Spirits of God.

And out of my spiritual body (out of the throne) came forth messages in various forms that were direct from God (lightening thundering and voices). These messages were to purify everything in me (seven lamps of fire burning) that was in the presence of my spiritual body (before the throne). This work of purification was being done by the Holy Spirit (seven Spirits of God).

Rev 4:6 And before the throne there was a sea of glass like unto crystal: and in the midst of the throne, and round about the throne, were four beasts full of eyes before and behind.

In the presence of my newly awakened spiritual body on which my spiritual mind and Christ were resting (and before the throne) the Bible became transparent to me in that I could see down into the depths of the Word as never before (there was a sea of glass). Portions of the Word I had never been able to understand were now opening before me (like unto crystal). Not only did my spirit understand the Word in depth, but my natural mind also understood because it was in close proximity to my spiritual mind.

Rev 4:7 And the first beast was like a lion, and the second beast like a calf, and the third beast had a face as a man, and the fourth beast was like a flying eagle.

At first (And the first) my natural body (beast) was in the imminent peril of death, (was like a lion), but it was now different than at first (and the second beast) because it was becoming younger. It was fresh, vigorous, strong, lively, and active (like a calf). My body was coming into divine completeness and perfection (and the third beast) but yet my outward appearance was that of a natural, ordinary person (had a face as a man). My natural body on earth (and the fourth beast) was rising up into a heavenly realm where death, sickness and aging could no longer affect me (was like a flying eagle).

Rev 4:8 And the four beasts had each of them six wings about him; and they were full of eyes within: and they rest not day and night, saying, Holy, holy, holy, Lord God Almighty, which was, and is, and is to come.

And the natural body (four beasts) had an imagination (six wings). This imagination had no limitations (full of eyes). It was able to praise God continually (rest not day and night). It knew that God was, always had been and always would be eternal God and holy in all his character and actions.

Rev 4:9-11 And when those beasts give glory and honor and thanks to him that sat on the throne, who liveth for ever and ever, the four and twenty elders fall down before him that sat on the throne, and worship him that liveth for ever and ever, and cast their crowns before the throne, saying, "Thou art worthy, O Lord, to receive glory and honor and power: for thou hast created all things, and for thy pleasure they are and were created."

When I worship God in my natural, conscious mind that dwells in my natural body (beasts) which is something I can do perpetually in my imagination, then my spiritual mind (twenty-four elders) also worships God in total submission (falling down before him in worship).

Revelation Five

Rev 5:1 And I saw in the right hand of him that sat on the throne a book written within and on the backside, sealed with seven seals.

I realized (saw) that I was trying to direct my own life by making decisions on my own rather than allowing Jesus to control my life (right hand of him who sat on the throne). I was trying to control my mind, my thoughts and my emotions (book in own hand) but I did not understand myself (written within) or my past (backside) as all the things I needed to understand about myself were unknown to me (sealed with seven seals).

Rev 5:2 And I saw a strong angel proclaiming with a loud voice, Who is worthy to open the book, and to loose the seals thereof?

And I understood (saw) from a difficult experience in my life (angel proclaiming in a loud voice) that someone needed to show me what was in my own heart (who is worthy to open the book) and reveal to me those things that I could not discover on my own (loose the seals thereof).

Rev 5:3 And no man in heaven, nor in earth, neither under the earth, was able to open the book, neither to look thereon.

And I realized there was no one in heaven nor in earth neither under the earth who was able to open my heart and see what was there.

Rev 5:4 And I wept much, because no man was found worthy to open and to read the book, neither to look thereon.

And I wept much because no one was found worthy to know what was in my heart.

Rev 5:5 And one of the elders saith unto me, Weep not: behold, the Lion of the tribe of Juda, the Root of David, hath prevailed to open the book, and to loose the seven seals thereof.

My spiritual mind caused me to understand (one of the elders) that Jesus (the Lion of the tribe of Judah, the Root of David), was able to disclose to me what was in my heart (prevailed to open the book) and set me free (loose the seven seals) from all that was therein (thereof).

Rev 5:6 And I beheld, and, lo, in the midst of the throne and of the four beasts, and in the midst of the elders, stood a Lamb as it had been slain, having seven horns and seven eyes, which are the seven Spirits of God sent forth into all the earth.

And I had the revelation (beheld and lo) that within the midst of my spiritual body (throne), my natural body (four beasts), and my spiritual mind (elders) was Jesus, the one who died for me (Lamb as it had been slain). I understood that he has perfect and complete (seven) power and knowledge (seven horns and seven eyes) and he is the perfect and complete (seven) Holy Spirit (seven Spirits of God) sent to me just as he promised his disciples that he would come (sent forth into all the earth).

Rev 5:7 And he came and took the book out of the right hand of him that sat upon the throne.

At this point Jesus took authority over my natural mind because I chose to hand it over to him. He took it out of my right hand which represents the place of power and control and now I no longer had that place of authority. Now Jesus would be the one sitting on the throne.

Rev 5:8 And when he had taken the book, the four beasts and four and twenty elders fell down before the Lamb, having every one of them harps, and golden vials full of odours, which are the prayers of saints.

When I gave Jesus authority over my natural mind (when Jesus had taken the book), Jesus was then on the throne of my life. This opened to me a new experience reserved for the church of the end times wherein when I would lie down, my natural body would feel the sensation of flying without actually leaving its physical environment, while my spiritual mind would focus on being in heaven with Jesus (the four beasts and the four and twenty elders fell down). There was the constant feeling of wavelike motion in my body. This was the Lord gently removing the sin nature from my body which would take place over a long period of time (harps). My thoughts were focused on Jesus as I expressed my love and appreciation for him in my holy imagination (prayers of the saints).

Rev 5:9 And they sung a new song, saying, Thou art worthy to take the book, and to open the seals thereof: for thou wast slain, and hast redeemed us to God by thy blood out of every kindred, and tongue, and people, and nation;

The people who have had this end-time experience of the awakening of the spiritual side of their being enabling them to experience God's presence and love continually will be able to worship God in a way never before possible (sung a new song). Jesus, because of who he is and what he has done for us (worthy), is able to reveal to us what is in our heart (take the book and open the seals). He is doing this for people all over the world (every kindred, tongue, people, and nation).

Rev 5:10 And hast made us unto our God kings and priests: and we shall reign on the earth.

God's faithful people will be so filled with his Spirit that they will reign on earth and minister according to his perfect will with no selfish motives or error.

Rev 5:11 And I beheld, and I heard the voice of many angels round about the throne and the beasts and the elders: and the number of them was ten thousand times ten thousand, and thousands of thousands;

Once Christ has become our very life, God is able to lift the veil and permit us to see and hear things in the heavenly realm that is nearby but has been hidden from our senses. We will see that there are more that are with us than those that are against us. We are surrounded by angels too numerous to count. Our physical body (four beasts) and our spiritual mind (24 elders) will also be in this heavenly dimension.

Rev 5:12 Saying with a loud voice, Worthy is the Lamb that was slain to receive power, and riches, and wisdom, and strength, and honour, and glory, and blessing.

As the veil is lifted and we see the angels in heaven, this verse shows us what they are doing. They are worshiping God. Although I believe this is probably going on continuously in heaven, they may be worshiping specifically in this passage related to the context of Rev 5 where a believer from the end times has been able to join with them in this worship because of the completed work of Christ in his life.

Rev 5:13 And every creature which is in heaven, and on the earth, and under the earth, and such as are in the sea, and all that are in them, heard I saying, Blessing, and honour, and glory, and power, be unto him that sitteth upon the throne, and unto the Lamb forever and ever.

As related to the context of this chapter, all things that have life can now be understood as having a significant purpose in the plan of God for this person's life and for all humanity. Now that this person is able to be in heaven with the veil lifted, he sees all of life as he has never seen it before. No longer does he separate creation or his own life into good and bad, but he sees all things from God's perspective. All things have had their place in the preparation of this person, as representative of the church of the end times, in order for him to come into completion in Christ. Therefore, all these things have been turned into praise because without adversity (as well as the good things), he could not be here.

Rev 5:14 And the four beasts said, Amen. And the four and twenty elders fell down and worshipped him that liveth forever and ever.

At last my physical body (four beasts) came into the perfection God intended for it as it aligned itself fully with all the scriptures related to the redemption of the body (said Amen). My spiritual mind (twenty four elders) was totally submitted to the will of God in complete humility such that it only wanted to fall down and worship God giving him full honor for all that he had done (worshiped him). I knew that because he lives forever and ever that I too would live forever because his life had become my life.

Revelation Six

Rev 6:1 And I saw when the Lamb opened one of the seals, and I heard, as it were the noise of thunder, one of the four beasts saying, Come and see.

I realized that Jesus (Lamb) had come to me and opened something within me that had been sealed off from me (one of the seals). This new thing opened to me was the slow, continuous and gentle movement of my spiritual body (noise of thunder) that was within my natural body (four beasts). This new experience was communicating something to me (come and see).

Rev 6:2 And I saw, and behold a white horse: and he that sat on him had a bow; and a crown was given unto him: and he went forth conquering, and to conquer.

I understood that my spiritual body had been awakened (I saw and behold a white horse). I also understood that Jesus who had come to me in this way was going to do a deeper work in my life to make me into the simplest fabric so he could form me into a perfect human being (and he that sat on him had a bow). I had given him authority over my life to do this (a crown was given unto him), and he was coming to conquer everything in me of my sinful nature that kept me from being able to enter his kingdom (he went forth conquering and to conquer).

Rev 6:3, 4 And when he had opened the second seal, I heard the second beast say, Come and see. And there went out another horse that was red: and power was given to him that sat thereon to take peace from the earth, and that they should kill one another: and there was given unto him a great sword.

When Jesus opened my understanding again (opened the second seal) I felt a different message in my body (second beast say, Come and see). This message was about division and difference regarding my bodies. I knew I had a body that was very different from my spiritual body. This other body was my natural body that had many needs and weaknesses (red horse) that often caused me to worry over whether or not my needs would be met (take peace from the earth.) I could feel that my natural body with all its needs and weakness was being separated from my spiritual body by a great sword in the hand of Jesus (given to him a great sword).

Rev 6:5 And when he had opened the third seal, I heard

the third beast say, Come and see. And I beheld, and lo a black horse; and he that sat on him had a pair of balances in his hand.

And when Jesus opened my understanding about how I would come into completion and divine perfection (opened the third seal) the understanding came in the form of messages received from my body (heard the third beast say, Come and see). I began to feel unpleasant things in my body (black horse) that were in direct correlation to my disobedience to God (he that sat on him had a pair of balances in his hand).

Rev 6:6 And I heard a voice in the midst of the four beasts say, A measure of wheat for a penny, and three measures of barley for a penny; and see thou hurt not the oil and the wine.

I heard God speak to me (I heard a voice) through my body (midst of the four beasts) placing limitations on what I was permitted to do in all areas of my life (a measure of wheat for a penny, and three measures of barley for a penny); there were no limitations placed on anything I did pertaining to the things of the Holy Spirit (hurt not the oil and the wine).

Rev 6:7 And when he had opened the fourth seal, I heard the voice of the fourth beast say, Come and see.

Jesus opened my understanding about something having to do with the weakness, helplessness and vanity (fourth) of my body (beast).

Rev 6:8 And I looked, and behold a pale horse: and his

name that sat on him was Death, and Hell followed with him. And power was given unto them over the fourth part of the earth, to kill with sword, and with hunger, and with death, and with the beasts of the earth.

After Jesus opened the fourth seal, I saw a part of my body that was subject to weakness, helplessness and vanity (pale horse). This is what would cause me to die and go to the grave (his name that sat on him was Death and Hell followed with him). However, the power of death had been limited in that he could only kill the condition in me of weakness, helplessness and vanity (fourth part of the earth) and nothing else. This death would be accomplished by the Word of God (Jesus) separating this weak part out from the rest of my body as in Heb 4:12 (the sword). My part was to cooperate with God by obeying instructions that would lead to the starvation of this condition of weakness (with hunger). Then death itself would die (and with death) as mortality was swallowed up by life (beasts of the earth).

Rev 6:9 And when he had opened the fifth seal, I saw under the altar the souls of them that were slain for the word of God, and for the testimony which they held:

Jesus revealed to me something about the redemption of my soul (when he had opened the fifth seal). I could see that because of my willingness to obey his Word by following Jesus, denying myself and taking up my cross (slain for the word of God), I was different. My life had become a testimony for others to see how Jesus can change a person's life (for the testimony which they held).

Rev 6:10 And they cried with a loud voice, saying, How

long, O Lord, holy and true, dost thou not judge and avenge our blood on them that dwell on the earth?

The parts of me that had experienced death to self eagerly desired to enter into the fullness of Christ. It was difficult to wait for other parts that were still dwelling in their carnal, earthly state to go through their death to self as well.

Rev 6:11 And white robes were given unto every one of them; and it was said unto them, that they should rest yet for a little season, until their fellowservants also and their brethren, that should be killed as they were, should be fulfilled.

The parts that were so eager to move into the fullness of Christ (previous verse) were comforted by God in knowing that even though they were fully sanctified (white robes) they should rest and enjoy their cleansed state for a little while longer (a little season) while they wait for the rest of their self (fellow servants) and their fellow Christians (brethren) to also come to the same state of purity (killed as they were).

Rev 6:12 And I beheld when he had opened the sixth seal, and, lo, there was a great earthquake; and the sun became black as sackcloth of hair, and the moon became as blood;

When Jesus revealed to me my sin showing how far short I was from the standard of perfection in Jesus Christ (opening the sixth seal), I went through a great trial (a great earthquake). I totally lost all perception of the presence of Jesus in my life (sun became black as sackcloth of hair). All

I could do was hold onto faith (moon) for my very life (blood).

Rev 6:13 And the stars of heaven fell unto the earth, even as a fig tree casteth her untimely figs, when she is shaken of a mighty wind.

Church leaders and doctrines I had trusted fell in my eyes (the stars of heaven fell unto the earth) as they now seemed to be immature and no longer applicable to what I was learning to be true about God and his church (as a fig tree casteth her untimely figs). This was because of the great infilling of the Holy Spirit I was experiencing (when she is shaken of a mighty wind).

Rev 6:14 And the heaven departed as a scroll when it is rolled together; and every mountain and island were moved out of their places.

And the heavenly realm where God and his holy angels dwell (heaven) was opening to me based on the negative messages in my DNA being transformed into the perfection God always intended to be in my DNA (as a scroll when it is rolled together). And pride (every mountain) was being removed from my life along with the fragmentation (island) caused by all the times I separated from myself, God and others.

Rev 6:15, 16 And the kings of the earth, and the great men, and the rich men, and the chief captains, and the mighty men, and every bondman, and every free man, hid themselves in the dens and in the rocks of the mountains; And said to the mountains and rocks, Fall on us, and hide us from the face of him that sitteth on the throne, and from the wrath of the Lamb:

Just as rich and influential people give plans and instructions for others to carry out, even so our DNA gives instructions to control the actions of the cells of our body. The people are evil which is evident because they want to hide from God. There is evil in our DNA that contains the curse of death put upon all living things at the time of the Fall. We know that just as people cannot hide to escape God's judgment neither can the DNA that contains the curse of death hide from God.

Rev 6:17 For the great day of his wrath is come; and who shall be able to stand?

We are living in the Day of the Lord and great judgments are even now coming upon the entire world. These judgments will be so numerous and severe, we may wonder if any human beings can survive them.

Works Cited

Bonhoeffer, Dietrich. 1963. *Ethics*. The Macmillan Company.

Bonner, John Tyler. (2014, June 10). Reproduction. Retrieved February 19, 2016 from http://www.britannica.com/science/reproduction-biology

Bullinger, E. W. 1967. *Number in Scripture*. Grand Rapids: Kregel Publications.

Katz, Authur. 1999. *Apostolic Foundations*. Burning Bush Publications, a ministry of Ben Israel Fellowship.

Nee, Watchman. 1992. *The Spiritual Man* Vol 1. Anaheim: Living Stream Ministry.

Rafael. (2009, January 24). DNA Structure: Hydrogen Bonds. Retrieved February 19, 2016 from http://www.brighthub.com/science/genetics/articles/23384.aspx

Rouse, Margaret. (2005 September). Sound Waves. Retrieved January 29, 2016 from http://whatis.techtarget.com/definition/sound-wave

About the Author

Patricia Baird Clark has long been an ardent studier of God's Word. Convinced that reading the Word instead of studying it may stunt our spiritual growth, she demonstrates this belief with her many deep Bible studies and teachings. As of this writing, many of these teachings have gone out to thousands via her website articles, books and YouTube videos. The Holy Spirit has taught her a unique approach to study that goes beneath the historical account to reveal the inner workings of the human soul and spirit. In this way ancient history is brought up to date because the human psyche is the same today as it has been since the beginning of history. In conjunction with her studies has been a decades-long ministry to severely abused and dissociated persons who, she has learned, are often living illustrations of what she has seen in Scripture. The interactions of dissociated parts with each other, with demons, and with God have been powerful models of the truths of Scripture in action.

Patricia is a graduate of the University of Indianapolis and has served in pastoral ministry alongside her husband, Dr. F. Stoner Clark, for over forty years. The Clarks reside in a small cabin located in the mountains of Western New York. They have two daughters and six grandchildren living in other states.

www.ingramcontent.com/pod-product-compliance
Lightning Source LLC
LaVergne TN
LVHW051547070426
835507LV00021B/2446